Cambridge Elements

Elements in Ancient and Pre-modern Economies
edited by
Kenneth Hirth
Pennsylvania State University
Timothy Earle
Northwestern University
Emily J. Kate
University of Vienna

ANCIENT AND PRE-MODERN ECONOMIES OF THE NORTH AMERICAN PACIFIC NORTHWEST

Anna Marie Prentiss
University of Montana

CAMBRIDGE
UNIVERSITY PRESS

Shaftesbury Road, Cambridge CB2 8EA, United Kingdom

One Liberty Plaza, 20th Floor, New York, NY 10006, USA

477 Williamstown Road, Port Melbourne, VIC 3207, Australia

314–321, 3rd Floor, Plot 3, Splendor Forum, Jasola District Centre, New Delhi – 110025, India

103 Penang Road, #05–06/07, Visioncrest Commercial, Singapore 238467

Cambridge University Press is part of Cambridge University Press & Assessment, a department of the University of Cambridge.

We share the University's mission to contribute to society through the pursuit of education, learning and research at the highest international levels of excellence.

www.cambridge.org
Information on this title: www.cambridge.org/9781009343466

DOI: 10.1017/9781009343480

First published 2023

A catalogue record for this publication is available from the British Library.

ISBN 978-1-009-34346-6 Paperback
ISSN 2754-2955 (online)
ISSN 2754-2947 (print)

Cambridge University Press & Assessment has no responsibility for the persistence or accuracy of URLs for external or third-party internet websites referred to in this publication and does not guarantee that any content on such websites is, or will remain, accurate or appropriate.

Ancient and Pre-modern Economies of the North American Pacific Northwest

Elements in Ancient and Pre-modern Economies

DOI: 10.1017/9781009343480
First published online: February 2023

Anna Marie Prentiss
University of Montana

Author for correspondence: Anna Marie Prentiss, anna.prentiss@umontana.edu

Abstract: This Element provides an overview of pre-modern and ancient economies of the Pacific Northwest region of North America. The region is widely known for its densely occupied semisedentary villages, intensive production economies, dramatic ritual life, and complex social relations. Scholars recognize significant diversity in the structure of subsistence and goods production in the service of domestic groups and institutional entities throughout the region. Here, domestic and institutional economies, specialization, distribution, economic development, and future directions are reviewed. The Element closes with thoughts on the processes of socio-economic change on the scales of houses, villages, and regional strategies.

Keywords: Pacific Northwest region, ancient and pre-modern economies, food producers, potlatch, cultural evolution

ISBNs: 9781009343466 (PB), 9781009343480 (OC)
ISSNs: 2754-2955 (online), 2754-2947 (print)

Contents

1 Introduction and Historical Background

This Element provides an introduction to the ancient and pre-modern economies of the greater Pacific Northwest region of North America. The greater Pacific Northwest region (Figures 1 and 2) is famous in the anthropological literature for its subsistence economies based heavily on fishing and the elaborate production activities in service of high-density settlements, long-distance exchange, feasting, and potlatching or ritualized gifting ceremonies (e.g. Boas 1897; Drucker 1955; Suttles 1968). Consequently, the cultures of the Indigenous groups of the Pacific Northwest (Figure 3) have long been of central interest to economic and ecological anthropologists (e.g. Ellen 1982; Forde 1963; Harris 1968; Herskovits 1952; Hirth 2020). Multiple major synthetic works on Pacific Northwest archaeology and ethnology have also been written (Ames and Maschner 1999; Matson and Coupland 1995; Moss 2011; Prentiss and Kuijt 2004; Suttles 1990a; Walker 1998).

My first goal is to provide a comparative synthesis of socio-economic variability that draws from the ethnographic and archaeological records of the Pacific Northwest region. I begin with the domestic economy. To accomplish this, I provide a short review of the geographic and ecological context for the Northwest Coast and Plateau and then follow with reviews of variation in subsistence economies and household organization. I draw extensively on the ethnographic record of the region as it provides a rich source of information that cannot be matched with archaeological data alone. Archaeological data provide selective backup and unique insights into long-term history. This permits me to comment on variability in the logic of interfamily labor and differential contributions to their residential groups, spanning simple family bands on the eastern Plateau to formal house groups on many portions of the Coast. I then address the institutional economy in which we find a diverse array of strategies by which groups managed land, resources, production, exchange, kin relations, warfare, and ritual events. I make distinctions between groups with autonomous villages but lacking clans, autonomous villages with clans, and multi-village political units variously identified as local groups, tribes, confederacies, and chiefdoms. I also comment on diversity in secret societies, an essential element among many Coastal groups for maintaining and growing power while celebrating sacred beliefs. The logical next step is to consider the structure of production and distribution as directed from within domestic and institutional contexts. The topic of specialization is a critical one in the Pacific Northwest region as crafting and other occupational specializations are well known. Individuals were rarely true full-time specialists within one house, village, or wider

Figure 1 Map of the greater Pacific Northwest region showing major coastlines, mountain ranges, river systems, and modern political boundaries.

political unit, meaning that they often also engaged in subsistence and related activities. This has led to concepts of embedded specialists (Ames 1995) to explain the transitory and variable nature of these positions. All members of Pacific Northwest societies produced food and goods, which were distributed within and well beyond individual houses and villages. I review two major forms of distribution: exchange and ritual gifting. Pacific Northwest societies maintained extensive exchange networks, with some communities developing as

Figure 2 Map of the Pacific Northwest region depicting subregions discussed in the text.

major trade centers. Good examples include the Metlakhatla Tsimshian, Lillooet (St'át'imc; see Table 1), and Lower Chinookan villages. Potlatching or highly ritualized gifting and feasting was widely practiced on the Central and North Coasts and to a limited degree elsewhere. Measuring the development of these traditions in the archaeological record remains challenging, yet there have been a number of breakthrough studies supporting arguments that core elements of Northwest Coast and Plateau culture appeared in substantially integrated form

1 Klamath and Modoc
2 Molala
3 Western Columbia River Sahaphins
4 Wasco, Wishram, and Cascades
5 Cayuse, Umatilla, and Walla Walla
6 Nez Perce
7 Yakima and Neighboring Groups
8 Palouse
9 Couer d'Alene
10 Spokane
11 Middle Columbia River Salish
12 Kalispel
13 Northern Okanagan, Sinixt, and Colville
14 Nicola
15 Nlaka'pamux
16 Lillooet
17 Secwepemc
18 Haihais
19 Haisla
20 Haida
21 Eyak
22 Tlingit
23 Tsimshian
24 Gitksan
25 Nishga
26 Heiltsuk
27 Nuxalk
28 W'ui'kinoxv
29 Kwakwaka'wakw
30 Northern Coast Salish
31 Nuu-chah-nulth
32 Makah
33 Central Coast Salish
34 Quileute
35 Southern Coast Salish
36 Kwalhioqua
37 Southwestern Coast Salish
38 Chinookans
39 Clatskanie
40 Tillamook
41 Alseans
42 Shualawans
43 Coosans
44 Athapaskans
45 Takelina
46 Kalapuyans
47 Chemakum

St'át'imc, Lil'wat

Wenatchi, Sanpoil

Klallam, Cowichan, Lummi, Squamish

Puyallup, Twana

Quinault

Sources: Esri, HERE, Garmin, Intermap, increment P Corp., GEBCO, USGS, FAO, NPS, NRCAN, GeoBase, IGN, Kadaster NL, Ordnance Survey, Esri Japan, METI, Esri China (Hong Kong) (c) OpenStreetMap contributors, and the GIS User Community

Figure 3 Map of the Pacific Northwest region depicting general territories of Indigenous groups as known from the nineteenth century.

by the Middle Holocene. Recent outcomes challenge us to think carefully about the means by which ancient economies evolved in the short and long term.

My second goal is to introduce new explanatory arguments concerning socio-economic diversity from long- and short-term standpoints. Explanation of diversity in Pacific Northwest economies is challenging given their high variation. On one extreme, we see groups on the outer Central and North

Table 1 List of Indigenous groups showing common names and contemporary versions used in this Element. Numbers reference those designations in Figure 3.

Map Designation	Common Name	Contemporary Name(s)
13	Lakes	Sinixt
15	Thompson	Nlaka'pamux
16	Lillooet	Lil'wat (Lower Lillooet)
		St'át'imc (Upper Lillooet)
17	Shuswap	Secwepemc
26	Bella Bella	Heiltsuk
27	Bella Coola	Nuxálk
28	Oowekeeno	W'ui'kinoxv
29	Kwakiutl	Kwakwaka'wakw
31	Nootka	Nuu-chah-nulth

Coast with locally dense and substantially sedentary populations with guarded territories supported by intense harvesting of fish, shellfish, sea mammals, terrestrial mammals, and a diverse range of plants. These groups had long-lived Houses (often identified as lineage groups) that were often members of multi-village political entities with sometimes cross-cutting clan affiliations. Specialist production of material goods played a major role in the acquisition of nonlocal resources and in complex rituals requiring lavish gifts (potlatches) to invited guests for purposes of validating new statuses and demonstrating the strength of the associated House and larger social group. On the other extreme, there were many groups in the Interior Northwest (Plateau) who maintained relatively frequent residential moves with minimally guarded annual ranges and supported by a diverse subsistence base that included terrestrial game, freshwater and anadromous fish, and intensive harvesting and processing of plant foods spanning geophytes (roots) and berries to a variety of seeds. These groups generally did not support craft specialists or host potlatches, yet they participated in extended trade networks with those who did maintain such elements. Explanation of regional variability requires theoretical concepts capable of incorporating ecological, demographic, and social variables. I argue that multi-model scenarios drawn from evolutionary ecology are particularly useful in anticipating such variation across the diverse land- and seascapes of the greater Pacific Northwest.

As discussed in greater detail in Section 5, my argument is that demographic ecological factors played a critical role in constraining cultural diversity throughout the region. In essence, groups settled into geographically constrained contexts lacked mobility options as alternatives during subsistence crises. This created a socio-environmental context that favored the development of elaborate cultural traditions (feasts and potlatches, for example) designed to ensure favorable political relationships with neighbors and to attract and retain group members as a response to inevitable losses (Ames 2006). In contrast, groups lacking such landscape-level constraints substituted residential mobility and subsistence extensification for competitive economic and demographic signaling, thus reducing the chance that dramatic social events would be practiced. Demonstrating the logic of this argument requires an examination of the full range of societies and associated cultural traditions from the region, thus my use of case material from the entire Northwest Coast and Plateau. It is also important to retain the Plateau in these discussions as Indigenous groups of the Plateau maintained critical direct and indirect exchange relationships with their neighbors on the Coast, spoke common languages (primarily variations of Salish and Sahaptin), and maintained many common cultural traditions.

Scholars recognize that the economies of the Pacific Northwest have a deep and complex history (Moss 2011). To fully understand that history, we need to move beyond ecological models to consider long-term evolutionary processes. I close this Element with an argument that Northwest Coast Indigenous groups crossed a major threshold in cultural evolution, approximating what evolutionary biologists term a "great transition" (Szathmary and Maynard Smith 1995). In essence, groups on the Coast transformed their societies from egalitarian, family-centered, and residentially mobile to semisedentary, nonegalitarian House or lineage-based groups. In accomplishing this, they altered the major locus of selection from person and family to House and village unit. They substantially increased the number of at least part-time specialist positions. Finally, they clearly instituted new communication systems in the form of the first Northwest Coast style of "art" forms. This served as the platform on which subsequent regional innovations were added, thus leading to the range of variation later recognized ethnographically. However, the archaeological record makes it clear that there was similar if not greater variation across the region as early as 4,000–5,000 years ago and that cultural change was regionally divergent and uneven (Clark 2010).

2 Domestic Economy

Hirth (2020: 17) defines the domestic economy as "the full array of provisioning activities carried out by the co-resident household or family unit for its social and biological maintenance." In order to fully appreciate the diversity of approaches to Indigenous domestic economy in the Pacific Northwest, I need to provide background on the geographic and ecological context, fundamental subsistence strategies, and variation in the organization of household production throughout the region. Thus, in this section, I introduce the ecological context and resource distributions for the greater Pacific Northwest. After introducing the geography and ecology of the greater Pacific Northwest, I then explore the domestic economy in two ways. First, I review variation in annual subsistence and mobility cycles. Second, I examine variation in household cooperation and its implication for the organization of labor and the distribution of food and other goods.

2.1 Geographic and Ecological Context

For purposes of this study, the greater Pacific Northwest region consists of the Northwest Coast, stretching from the Copper River Delta, Alaska, south to the Chetco River Mouth, Oregon (Suttles 1990b), along with the Interior Northwest (also known as the Plateau region), consisting of the landscape associated with the eastern Cascade and Coast Ranges, Blue–Ochoco Mountains, Columbia Basin, Okanagan Highlands, Fraser–Thompson Plateau, and western foothills of the Rocky Mountains (Chatters 1998) (Figure 1). The diverse ecosystems of the Pacific Northwest are affected by climate, physiography, the sea, and human management. Weather across the region is affected by two atmospheric pressure cells, the Pacific High and the Aleutian Low. The counterclockwise-circulating Aleutian Low is centered over the Bering Sea but expands in the fall to cover a large portion of the North Pacific, bringing cyclonic storms with significant moisture to the entire Pacific Northwest region. While the Aleutian Low brings storms to the entire region in winter, it is responsible for significant moisture in the northern portion of the Coast throughout the year. In contrast, the subtropical Pacific High is centered to the south off the California Coast in winter but can expand in the summer, bringing clockwise-circulating winds to the region. Winter storms are not uncommon and spring storms circulate ocean-floor nutrients, initiating the warm season growth cycle.

The physiography of the region is defined by a series of subregions identified by Suttles (1990b) as the Pacific Border, Cascade and Coastal Ranges, Intermontane (including the Fraser–Columbia Plateau), and the Rocky–Cassiar–Columbia Mountains (Rockies). As noted by Chatters (1998), the north–south trending mountain ranges of the Pacific Border, Cascade and Coastal, and Rockies subregions serve to block moist air masses moving in from the west, leading to the release of moisture (rain or snow) on the western slopes and peak areas. As the air flow moves across the mountains and filters into the Intermontane regions, it increases in temperature and the ability to hold moisture. This in turn favors more arid conditions east of the Cascade and Coastal zone and again east of the Rockies. Moisture is drained by several major systems, along with many smaller streams and rivers. The Fraser and Columbia River systems drain the majority of the Plateau and portions of the Central and South Coasts. The Bella Coola, Skeena, Nass, and Stikine Rivers drain much of the North Coast. Rivers are important for many reasons, including as conduits for seasonal spawning of anadromous fish and as travel corridors for human groups.

Sea conditions are also a critical factor affecting ecological variability across the region. Two major currents affect sea temperatures. The cold subarctic current flows west to east, splitting off the coast of Vancouver Island and forming the Alaska Current heading north and the California Current moving south. This current system is pushed offshore during the winter by the warmer Davison Current that originates off Baja, California. Sea surface temperatures affect variation in sea life, with colder water favoring greater productivity. In general, temperatures are colder to the north but vary to some degree with seasons. Tidal cycles are complex but generally characterized by two lows and two highs per day, with variability in strength dependent upon lunar cycles (Suttles 1990b). Tidal changes can be especially dramatic where channels are narrow. Finally, salinity affects marine resources. Brackish water around river mouths does not favor shellfish growth. However, deep inlets along the coast can have enough salt content to permit substantial populations of saltwater fish (Suttles 1990b).

The vegetation of the Northwest Coast varies substantially in relation to moisture. The North Coast is dominated by the Sitka spruce–western hemlock zone, which grades to a narrow band on the outer portion of the South Coast. The western hemlock–Douglas fir zone dominates the South and portions of the Central Coast. The Central and South Coasts also include the extensive forests of the mountain hemlock–silver fir zone (Suttles 1990b). The more arid Plateau is characterized by a patchwork of vegetative zones, including the shrub and bunchgrass steppes of the Columbia Basin and canyons of the Fraser and Thompson Rivers as well as the xeric, mesic, and subalpine forests of the eastern Cascades/Coastal Ranges, Okanagan highlands, and western Rockies (Chatters 1998). Human groups managed their environments to enhance productivity by the use of fire (opening the forests for hunting and enhancing productivity of select economically valuable species) (Turner 2014) and directly growing select plant foods such as wapato (Hoffmann et al. 2016; Lyons et al. 2021).

2.2 Animal and Plant Resources of the Greater Pacific Northwest

Fish played an outsized role in most traditional economies across the greater Pacific Northwest region and can be divided into saltwater, anadromous, and freshwater species. Saltwater fish are numerous and span deeper water species such as tuna (*Thunus* sp.), halibut (*Hippoglossus stenolepis*), and cods (various taxa) to a range of smaller taxa often obtained in inshore waters, including rockfish (*Sebastes* sp.), herring (*Clupea harengus*), smelt (*Hypomesus pretiosus*), capelin (*Mallotus villosus*), skates (*Raja* sp.), dog-fish sharks (*Squalas acanthius*), sculpins (Cottidae), and small flatfishes (Pleuronectidae).

Anadromous fish were seasonally productive in coastal waters and rivers throughout the region. They include five salmon species (Chinook [*Oncorhynchus tshawytsa*], sockeye [*Oncorhynchus nerka*], coho [*Oncorhynchus kisutch*], pink [*Oncorhynchus gorbuscha*], and chum or dog [*Oncorhynchus keta*]). Other anadro-mous fish include steelhead trout (*Salmon garidneri*) and eulachon or candlefish (*Thaleichthys pacificus*). Chinook (also known as spring and king) salmon are spring to early summer spawners and tend to run deep in river channels. Sockeye runs occur in mid-to-late summer and can be caught at shallow depths. Both of the latter have long runs up the major rivers, with sockeye also requiring upstream lakes to complete the spawning process (Quinn 2005). In contrast, the later spawning pink, coho, and chum salmon tend to have much shorter runs and generally do not make it past the lower portions of the major river systems (Quinn 2005). Chinook and sockeye salmon and eulachon were particularly valued for their higher fat content. Schalk (1977) notes that high annual discharge stability (rivers), lower temperatures, higher precipitation, and lower evapotranspiration as recognized for the North and Central Coast were most positive for stable and populous spawning cycles.

Invertebrates were selectively managed and harvested across the greater Pacific Northwest. The greatest variety naturally occur on the Coast and include those attached to or associated with rocks (various mussels [*Mytilus* sp.], scallops (*Hinnites multirugosus*], oysters [*Ostrea lurida*], cockles [*Cardium corbis*], abalone [*Haliotis kamtschatkana*], barnacles [*Balanus glandula* and *Mitella polymerus*], and urchins [*Strongylocentrotus* sp.]), bur-ied in sand (clams [e.g. *Schizothaerus* sp.]), open shallow water (crabs [*Cancer* sp.], sea cucumber [*Stichopus californicus*], and octopus [*Octopus appollyon*]), and deeper water shellfish (e.g. dentalium [*Dentalium preto-sium*]) (Quayle 1960; Suttles 1990b). Lepofsky et al. (2015) document sig-nificant investment in the creation of "clam beds" to foster greater bivalve production at select locales on the Central Coast. Invertebrates were generally less important on the Plateau. Where used, invertebrate taxa included freshwater mussels (*Margaritifera falcata* and *Gonidea angulata*), along with some crayfish and insects (Chatters 1998).

Mammals divide into marine and terrestrial groups (Cowan and Guiguet 1973). Marine mammals were a critical resource for Indigenous groups along the Coast. Harbor seals (*Phoca vitulina*) and northern sea lions (*Eumetopias jubatus*) are found throughout the region. Harbor seals are found in marine contexts but also well up some major rivers, including Harrison Lake in the Fraser Valley. A variety of porpoises and whales inhabit the Coast, though some such as humpback (*Megaptera novaeangliae*) and gray (*Eschrichtius gibbosus*) whales are seasonal migrants. Finally, sea otters (*Enhyda lutris*) were formerly common throughout the Coast region. Terrestrial taxa were pursued in both the Coast and Plateau regions. Deer species (*Odocoileus* sp.) are most common in Douglas fir and parkland forests and in some steppe environments. Elk or wapiti (*Cervus elaphus*) exist on the Central and South Coasts and in more mountainous terrain on the Plateau. Two species of mountain sheep (*Ovis* sp.) are found in generally mountainous contexts as are mountain goats (*Oreamnos americanus*). Moose (*Alces alces*) are generally found in interior montane environments. Finally, more arid contexts favor pronghorn antelope (*Antilocapra americana*) and bison (*Bison bison*), the latter albeit in low numbers. Black and brown bears (*Ursus* sp.) are found throughout the region as are a multitude of carnivores ranging from small (e.g. ermines, otters, martens) to larger predators such as wolves (*Canis lupus*) and mountain lions (*Felis concolor*) (Chatters 1998; Suttles 1990b).

A diverse range of birds inhabit the greater Pacific Northwest (Chatters 1998; Munro and Cowan 1947; Suttles 1990b). Economically important birds include migratory ducks and geese, some known to congregate in select areas of the Plateau, for example at Klamath Lakes (Chatters 1998). Suttles (1990b) notes that breeding colonies of seabirds were an economically important source of both birds and eggs. A range of ground birds including various grouse, ptarmigan, and quail taxa were important, particularly on the Plateau. Finally, a number of birds of prey provided nonfood resources including feathers, claws, and bones (used for beads and drinking tubes).

Turner (2014) provides an exhaustive review of plants in traditional Pacific Northwest economies. Edible plant taxa include those with edible rhizomes, tubers, and bulbs (geophytes); berries and fruits; greens; nuts and seeds; cambium; and lichens and moss. I highlight several critical taxa. Silverweed (*Potentilla pacifica*) and wapato (*Sagittaria latifolia*) were managed (Turner et al. 2021) and in some cases gardened in portions of the Coast (Hoffmann et al. 2016). Other critical geophytes included camas (*Camassia* sp.) and spring beauty (*Claytonia lanceolata*), both used on the Plateau. A great array of berry species were harvested and consumed, including gooseberries (*Ribes* sp.), members of the rose (e.g. *Rubus* sp., *Rosa* sp., *Amelanchier alnifolia*) and heather (*Vaccinium* sp., *Arctostaphylos uva-ursi*) families, elderberries (*Sambucus* sp.), and soap berries (*Shepherdia canadensis*). Edible cambium was acquired from select tree species and often used in times of food shortages. Turner (1998) also documents the range of plants used in traditional technologies across the region. A variety of woods, the most famous being western red cedar, were used for manufacturing houses, monuments (poles), hand tools (e.g. bowls, ladles, rattles, masks, handles, shafts for weapons and digging sticks), and canoes. Bark was used for ropes, masks, and baskets. Roots (especially spruce root) and grasses were used for weaving.

2.3 Land Use, Subsistence, and Mobility

We can gain insights into variation in annual subsistence and mobility cycles by exploring individual ethnographic cases that varied in terms of their relative investments in residential moves and emphases on fishing, hunting, and gathering (Figure 4). While it is widely known that many Pacific Northwest groups occupied stable winter villages, there was substantial reliance upon different combinations of residential and logistical mobility (per Binford 1980) depending upon resource configurations. One hallmark for all groups was intense engagement with the production of enough foods, particularly sources of fat and carbohydrates (Tushingham et al. 2021) to ensure winter and early spring survival. The need for winter storage was consistent throughout the region, though mediated by options for access to resources via winter mobility and food procurement.

Plateau groups are known for variable investments in fishing and a strong reliance on hunting and gathering. The Lillooet are made up of two groups, Lil'wat and St'át'imc, both residing on the western Plateau and eastern Coast Mountains of southern British Columbia (Teit 1906). The St'át'imc annual cycle began in late winter to early spring, when families began to leave winter villages in search of fresh food resources. Warm season residential mobility was quite high as family groups moved through their topographically diverse environment, positioning themselves for accessing critical food sources (Alexander 1992; Kennedy and Bouchard 1998a; Prentiss and Kuijt 2012; Teit 1906). Mid-spring brought groups to intermediate elevation valleys for deer hunting and geophyte gathering/processing. Excess dried meat and roots were then transported to canyon bottom camps for summer salmon fishing and berry collecting. Dried roots, salmon, deer, and berries were cached in the field camps and also

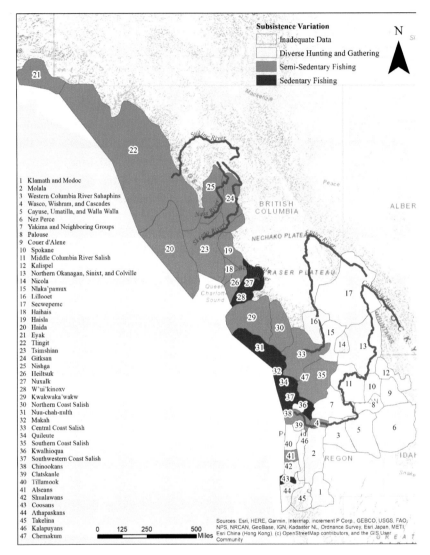

1 Klamath and Modoc
2 Molala
3 Western Columbia River Sahaphins
4 Wasco, Wishram, and Cascades
5 Cayuse, Umatilla, and Walla Walla
6 Nez Perce
7 Yakima and Neighboring Groups
8 Palouse
9 Couer d'Alene
10 Spokane
11 Middle Columbia River Salish
12 Kalispel
13 Northern Okanagan, Sinixt, and Colville
14 Nicola
15 Nlaka'pamux
16 Lillooet
17 Secwepemc
18 Haihais
19 Haisla
20 Haida
21 Eyak
22 Tlingit
23 Tsimshian
24 Gitksan
25 Nishga
26 Heiltsuk
27 Nuxalk
28 W'ui'kinoxv
29 Kwakwaka'wakw
30 Northern Coast Salish
31 Nuu-chah-nulth
32 Makah
33 Central Coast Salish
34 Quileute
35 Southern Coast Salish
36 Kwalhioqua
37 Southwestern Coast Salish
38 Chinookans
39 Clatskanle
40 Tillamook
41 Alseans
42 Shualawans
43 Coosans
44 Athapaskans
45 Takelina
46 Kalapuyans
47 Chemakum

Figure 4 Map of the Pacific Northwest region depicting variation in Indigenous subsistence and mobility strategies. Groups identified as fishing derive a large proportion of their diet from marine and anadromous resources (Binford 2001).

transported back to the winter village for storage. Finally, families headed back to the mountains for fall hunting, trout fishing, and harvesting of various plant foods before returning to winter villages in late fall. Winter survival required a complex system of food storage with below- and aboveground caches left in or near procurement camps, outdoors in the winter village, and within pithouse dwellings (Alexander 2000).

The Secwepemc groups are widely distributed across the eastern Plateau within British Columbia (Teit 1909). While those who resided near the St'át'imc in the Fraser Canyon were more winter sedentary with access to the abundant fisheries, many other Secwepemc family groups were more mobile, moving their residential bases across an extensive landscape during much of the year in order to access a diverse range of anadromous and freshwater fish, plant resources, and game. The Sanpoil and Nespelem of the mid-Columbia valley and associated landscape operated a similar annual mobility and subsistence cycle (Ray 1933) in which springtime foraging required a residential move to the appropriate geophyte gathering grounds. At this time, women would intensely harvest and process large quantities of these resources. The fishing season began in May and stretched throughout the summer. Berries were also intensively gathered in mid-to-late summer. Fall season was for hunting and further geophyte gathering. People established or returned to previous winter residences in mid-fall, relying on stored geophytes, berries, salmon, and meat from fall hunting for winter survival (Ray 1933). The Coeur d'Alene people live on the eastern fringe of the Plateau in the western foothills of the Rocky Mountains. Similar to the Secwepemc groups, their traditional annual cycle included a period during winter (approximately January and February) where residential mobility was infrequent given the adequate stored food from fall hunting and gathering (Teit 1930). The warm season cycle began approximately in March and brought frequent residential moves to facilitate fish trapping, followed later by geophyte digging and roasting. The summer season included final geophyte procurement, berry harvesting, and salmon fishing. Fall was largely dedicated to bison hunting in the eastern Rockies and Great Plains (Teit 1930: 59). The latter was likely only with access to horses during the Colonial period (Palmer 1998).

Many Coastal groups were highly sedentary and focused heavily on fishing. The Nuu-chah-nulth and Makah resided on the west coast of Vancouver Island (Nuu-chah-nulth) and northwest portion of Washington State (Makah). While there was some variation between the many groups, we can recognize some commonalities to their subsistence and mobility cycles (Drucker 1951; McMillan 1999). Many of these groups moved between winter villages in protected locations within river valleys and warm season villages located in outer coast contexts. The spring season found many groups moving to outer villages to fish for spring (Chinook or king) salmon and herring, to collect herring eggs, and to hunt for migrating waterfowl. By mid-summer, groups were generally all residing in outer coast villages and focused on fishing for halibut and cod and hunting sea mammals. Both involved complex procedures from technological standpoints and typically required lengthy offshore trips in large canoes. Whaling was an elite-directed activity and required extensive spiritual preparation. Despite the physical, mental, and spiritual investment, successful hunts were rare (Drucker 1951). Summer season also brought the collecting and processing of marine invertebrates and many plant foods including berries and geophytes. During late summer and early fall, groups moved back to their winter residences and focused on catching and processing sockeye and chum salmon. The winter season was sedentary, with groups residing in large multi-family winter houses and relying upon stores of sea mammal blubber/oil, dried halibut, salmon, and clams; geophytes; and berry cakes. Breaks in winter weather provided short opportunities for women to gather invertebrates and berries while others could undertake winter hunts for land mammals (bear, deer, and elk) (Drucker 1951; McMillan 1999).

Kwakwaka'wakw groups relied more on logistical mobility via canoes (e.g. Ames 2002) based in centrally located villages to acquire critical subsistence resources (Codere 1990). Early warm season resources included eulachon, herring, and spring (Chinook) salmon (Boas 1911–1914, 1966; Codere 1990). Major expeditions were organized to areas where these resources can be obtained in large quantities. Later in summer and early fall, trips were organized for accessing berries, sea mammals, halibut, salmon, clover roots, and terrestrial mammals including mountain goat (Boas 1911–1914; Codere 1990). Winter hunting for deer and elk was often practiced as was bear hunting using traps (Boas 1966). As with most other groups in the region, winter subsistence depended upon stored resources largely from warm season activities. Fish oil (especially eulachon) was rendered and kept in kelp tubes. Many dried foods were consumed after dipping in oil. Essential dried foods included clams and mussels, berry cakes, halibut, salmon, and herring roe, which were kept in large boxes and on house racks (Boas 1911–1914, 1966; Codere 1990).

Central Coast Salish groups (Northern Straits, Island, and Downriver Halkomelem, Nooksack, and Clallam) also positioned villages in locales optimal for a wide range of marine and terrestrial resources (Barnett 1955; Suttles 1960), sometimes accessed using canoe-based logistical mobility similar to other Northwest Coast groups (Ames 2002). Consequently, spring to early summer brought access to spring (Chinook) and coho salmon, herring, sea mammals, and geophytes. Mid-to-late summer resources included sockeye, pink, and coho salmon. Halibut and sturgeon were fished throughout the warm season. Sea mammals, deer, and bears were also typically hunted in warm season months. Barnett (1955) notes that some groups included winter hunts for mountain goats. Plant resources were acquired primarily in the warm season as well. Berries became available in mid-to-late summer (Turner 2014). Geophytes varied in the availability to different groups – for example, as noted by Suttles (1990b), wapato was a critical resource for Katzie (see also Hoffmann et al. 2016), while camas was more important for Northern Straits groups. Barnett (1955) notes that food processing during the warm season was often designed to develop winter stores. Thus, earth ovens were used to cook geophytes before they could be dried and stored. Oil from eulachons, various land and sea mammals, and dogfish was rendered by boiling and stored in stomach sacks. Salmon and herring eggs were dried in bladders of select mammals. Bear fat was stored in intestine coils. Salmon were wind dried and/or smoked for storage, wrapped in bundles, and kept in winter houses. Berries were boiled, dried, and saved as cake-like masses, stored in chests.

The Chinookan groups occupied the Lower Columbia and adjacent valleys and provide an example of bi-seasonal cycles similar to those of the Nuu-chah-nulth, with moves between winter and summer villages (Ellis 2013). The Chinookan spring cycle began with moving from winter villages in the Lower Columbia and Columbia Gorge to warm season residences generally in the Wapato Valley area. This provided the opportunity for the harvesting and processing of geophytes (especially camas), fishing for spring (Chinook) salmon and eels, and harvesting of oysters. Summer focused on salmon fishing and the frequent transportation of dried foods between warm season residences and winter villages. Fall included final salmon fishing, deer and elk hunting, and the harvesting of berries, nuts, and camas. The winter season was spent in permanent villages, intensely reliant upon stores of fish, meat from terrestrial mammals, and plant foods accumulated during the warm season (Ellis 2013).

Other groups were also heavily invested in fishing but employed slightly more frequent residential movements. De Laguna (1972) provides an account of the Yakutat Tlingit annual cycle. Springtime was busy following the winter thaw. In early spring, activities included sea otter hunting, eulachon and halibut fishing, geophyte and bark gathering and processing, the harvesting of herring spawn, and Chinook salmon fishing. In late spring to early summer, many traveled to seal hunting camps and also collected birds' eggs, seaweed, and early season berries. Late summer to early fall activities consisted of intensive berry harvesting, salmon fishing, last geophyte harvesting, and late fall mountain goat hunting. Winter was spent in villages relying on stored food obtained during the warm season. Some individuals went hunting during this time for bears, seals, and mountain goats. Haida annual cycles were somewhat variable but generally included early spring bird hunting and egg collecting from field camps on select islands, followed by late spring halibut and salmon fishing, which lasted throughout the summer. Depending on context, some groups also had a spring herring season. Summer to early fall was a critical time for berry collecting. Groups engaged in duck and geese hunting and bear and marten trapping during mid-fall. Winter survival was predicated on stored smoked fish, fish oil, berries, and sea/terrestrial mammal meat and fat (Blackman 1990).

Tsimshian groups of the northern British Columbia Coast (Prince Rupert Harbour area and adjacent landscapes) operated a seasonal cycle that included multiple residential contexts spread across the inland and coastal areas of their territory (Halpin and Seguin 1990; Martindale 2003). The Tsimshian cycle generally began with intensive eulachon harvesting and processing in late winter to early spring on the Nass River. Mid-spring was a time when people generally moved to outer coast residences to gather seaweed, fish for halibut, and harvest herring eggs. Late spring included spring (Chinook) salmon fishing and egg collecting. Later in the summer, families moved to salmon fishing sites along rivers to intercept massive spawning runs, though this period was also optimum for harvesting berries, geophytes, and green shoots from various plants. Once salmon season was complete, some groups moved into interior hunting camps for bears, marmots, and ungulates. The winter season was spent in protected winter villages reliant upon stores of dried halibut, salmon, geophytes, berries, and meat. Coupland et al. (2010) suggest that during pre-Colonial times salmon may have been a particularly critical subsistence item in Prince Rupert Harbour villages. Tushingham et al. (2021) suggest that if that was the case sources of fat (i.e. eulachon oil) and carbohydrates must have been at least equally important for protein metabolization. The Gitksan annual cycle was extremely similar, though replacing the coastal aspect with intensified hunting of bear, moose, marmot, and mountain goats (Halpin and Seguin 1990). Similarly, Stó:lō groups of the Fraser Valley in southern British Columbia moved between winter villages, summer salmon fishing and berry collecting camps, and fall hunting camps, accumulating stores of dried/smoked fish, berries, geophytes (especially wapato), and terrestrial mammal meat for winter use (Duff 1952).

Finally, there are outliers who were substantially sedentary but relied far more on hunting and gathering than the other sedentary groups. The Sinixt provide an interesting example (Kennedy and Bouchard 1998b; Teit 1930). The Sinixt or Lakes people occupied the Upper Columbia and Slocan River valleys of southeastern British Columbia and northeast Washington State. The Sinixt relied upon canoe mobility for summer trips to Kettle Falls for salmon fishing and trade (Goodale et al. 2022). However, given that salmon runs were poor within the core of Sinixt territory, there was a significant interest in hunting deer, moose, mountain goats, mountain sheep, bears, and a wide range of fur bearers. Plant resources included berries and select species of geophytes (especially bitterroot and avalanche lily corms). Winter survival was thus predicated on the storage of dried meat, fish (to a lesser degree), and plant foods.

2.4 Household Organization

An integral part of the domestic economy was household labor organization and food and goods distribution. Coupland et al. (2009) note that house groups and households provided the fundamental units of production and distribution in Northwest Coast economies. The same argument can be made for Plateau communities, though house groups as formal social entities were not consistently present (Prentiss et al. 2005; Prentiss et al. 2022; Prentiss et al. in press). Coupland et al. (2009) recognize an initial distinction between the house as a domicile and the House as "a corporate body holding an estate" (Lévi-Strauss 1982: 174). The latter represent long-lived social units that controlled rights to corporeal and non-corporeal property as associated with one or more physical domiciles (Gillespie 2000a, 2000b). In this view, Houses, also termed "personnes morales" by Lévi-Strauss (1979, 1982), form the organizing focus with regard to individual duties and obligations. Thus, in many situations on the Northwest Coast, economic ventures, whether specialized production, exchange, or ritualized gifting, were sanctioned, organized, and conducted by the House. The organization of family life in houses was affected by the nature of the House groups, which could be held within a single house (as domicile) or extend across multiple houses.

Coupland et al. (2009) divide house groups in the Pacific Northwest into those with communalist and collectivist social strategies. To Coupland et al. (2009), the true communalist strategy occurred in the highly stratified North Coast groups where in essence each house membership served the House itself. In practical reality, this meant that commoners or those without a formal title often provided surplus food and other goods to those of higher rank. Archaeologically, this strategy is reflected in houses with diverse activity areas surrounding a central communal activity space. The Haida "big house" at Masset provides an excellent example with its two-tiered living surface surrounding a large basal activity zone with a central hearth (Blackman 1990: 243).

In contrast, collectivist Houses consisted of multiple persons and families who operated their own domestic economies but cooperated with each other for their own good. The persistence of the domicile and the House was a byproduct of that cooperation. Several groups (Wakashan speakers) seem to have operated Houses in an intermediate fashion with rigid social hierarchies but with some residential flexibility depending upon kin networks. Archaeological expectations include redundant domestic activity areas with hearths and storage facilities positioned around the perimeter of the house with the center retained as common space. House 1 at Ozette in the Makah area provides a good archaeological example with ranked family spaces surrounding an open area possibly used on occasion for dances, feasts, and other events (Samuels 2006). In the following discussion, I draw on these distinctions to explore variation in household organization across the greater Pacific Northwest region (Figure 5).

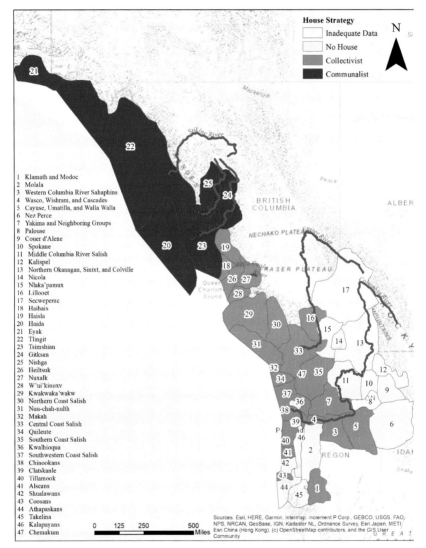

1 Klamath and Modoc
2 Molala
3 Western Columbia River Sahaphins
4 Wasco, Wishram, and Cascades
5 Cayuse, Umatilla, and Walla Walla
6 Nez Perce
7 Yakima and Neighboring Groups
8 Palouse
9 Couer d'Alene
10 Spokane
11 Middle Columbia River Salish
12 Kalispel
13 Northern Okanagan, Sinixt, and Colville
14 Nicola
15 Nlaka'pamux
16 Lillooet
17 Secwepemc
18 Haihais
19 Haisla
20 Haida
21 Eyak
22 Tlingit
23 Tsimshian
24 Gitksan
25 Nishga
26 Heiltsuk
27 Nuxalk
28 W'ui'kinoxv
29 Kwakwaka'wakw
30 Northern Coast Salish
31 Nuu-chah-nulth
32 Makah
33 Central Coast Salish
34 Quileute
35 Southern Coast Salish
36 Kwalhioqua
37 Southwestern Coast Salish
38 Chinookans
39 Clatskanle
40 Tillamook
41 Alseans
42 Shualawans
43 Coosans
44 Athapaskans
45 Takelina
46 Kalapuyans
47 Chemakum

Figure 5 Map of the Pacific Northwest region depicting variation in Indigenous household strategies. Collectivist and communalist groups maintained multigenerational social groups variously identified as Houses and Lineages (Coupland et al. 2009). The "No House" designation identified groups that did not maintain such long-lived social groups and thus lived in more flexible social situations with more ephemeral houses.

Plateau groups relied upon relatively frequent residential moves to position families with reference to various resources and to meet social obligations. Given the frequent residential movements and the need for group coresidential flexibility, houses tended to be occupied for limited spans of time, typically no more than a single season. Many groups had a distinction between more substantial winter residences (pithouses) and more ephemeral summer domiciles (mat lodges of various forms). Yet even more architecturally involved winter residences were not occupied for more than a few seasons. Indeed, some were deconstructed at the end of each season. Secwepemc groups constructed winter pithouses structured around a series of "rooms" such that there was a kitchen/storeroom and several others designed to facilitate movement, work, and sleeping quarters for the residents (Teit 1909). The archaeology of Secwepemc house pits indicates they were small (5–7 m in diameter), had central hearths, and, based upon the extent of accumulated rim middens, were probably not occupied for more than several seasons (Wilson and Carlson 1980). The central hearths and activity-specific "rooms" suggest that they were organizationally communalist though not representative of true Houses in the Lévi-Strauss sense. The Sanpoil constructed winter pithouses with central hearths and large winter mat lodges (Ray 1933). The latter were rectangular in form (in contrast to generally circular pithouses) and had room for two to eight families depending upon the size of the house. Pairs of families shared hearths and thus there could be as many as four hearth groups, suggesting a somewhat collectivist approach. However, since these structures were entirely dismantled at the end of winter there is nothing to suggest that residential groups functioned as a House per Lévi-Strauss. Okanagan, Sinixt, and Middle Columbia Salish groups (e.g. Wenatchi) appear to have operated very similar residence cycles and patterns of household organization (Miller 1998; Ray 1933; Teit 1930). Coeur d'Alene families spent the winter season in several kinds of structures designed for no more than single extended families (Teit 1930). These included conical mat lodges placed over shallowly excavated floors with the extra sediment packed around the lower walls of the structure, skin lodges similar to Great Plains tipis, and bark lodges. The bark lodges were oblong and designed to hold one to four families positioned around one to two hearths. Similar to Mid-Columbia groups, Coeur d'Alene groups also built mat-covered long lodges designed to hold larger aggregates of people during social gatherings. This diversity of house occupation patterns was largely responsive to local conditions, the resources available, and intended lengths of stay (Teit 1930) and none were long-lived. Thus, as elsewhere on the central and eastern Plateau, the family remained the basic unit of production and consumption.

A number of Interior and Coastal groups maintained true Houses and commonly organized them in a collectivist manner, though there is some interesting variation. Unlike many Plateau groups, frequency of residential moves was less important. Lillooet groups subdivide into the Lil'wat and the St'át'imc, the former closer to the Fraser Valley and the latter on the western Canadian Plateau and adjacent eastern Coast Range (Teit 1906). Both operated a bi-seasonal land-use strategy that included permanent winter residences in villages of various sizes. Lil'wat houses included aboveground wooden structures (Figure 6) organized in a way similar to many Coast Salish residences. St'át'imc and some Lil'wat groups occupied winter villages made up of arrangements of semi-subterranean pithouses (Figure 7). Houses among both groups ranged from small (about 5 m in diameter) with space for only one extended family to much larger houses (15 m or more in diameter) large enough for multiple families. Archaeological research suggests that larger St'át'imc houses could hold three to five families as indicated by redundant arrangements of hearths, cache pits, and kitchen debris around the house floor perimeter (Hayden 1997; Prentiss et al. 2022). Additionally, excavations at the large villages of Bridge River and Keatley Creek confirm that many houses accumulated deep rim middens and superimposed anthropogenic floors, with dated sequences of 350 or more years (Prentiss et al. 2022). Research at the deeply stratified Housepit 54 at Bridge River suggests that social strategies in long-occupied houses could evolve. Thus, as Housepit 54 grew in size it also shifted

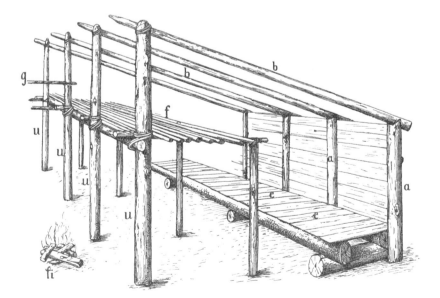

Figure 6 Interior of a Lower Lillooet (Lil'wat) collectivist house showing one of many single-family living spaces (Teit 1906: 214).

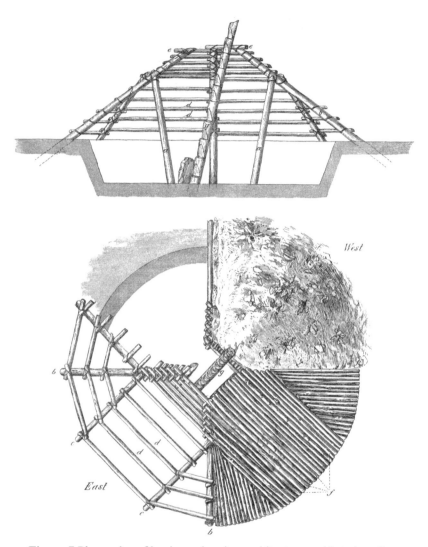

Figure 7 Plan and profile views showing architecture and interior of an
Nlaka'pamux pithouse (Teit 1900: 193).

from a communalist to a collectivist strategy (Prentiss et al., "Evolutionary
Household," 2020; Prentiss et al. 2022). Interestingly, during its reoccupation in
the late Fur Trade period (ca. 1852–1858 CE), Housepit 54 shifted back to
a communalist orientation (Williams-Larson et al. 2017). Smith (2017) documents
similar fluctuation in house floor organization at the Little S7istken site also located
in the Bridge River valley. Thus, it is clear that Lillooet villages were socially
organized around long-lived Houses, with houses occupied by groups mostly using
collectivist strategies but some cooperating communally as well.

Scholars also recognize variation in Central Coast Salish groups (e.g. Stó:lō, Squamish, Cowichan, and Klallam). Suttles (1990d) notes that families occupied their own spaces within winter houses as marked by spatially distinct fires and storage facilities. Suttles (1990d: 464) also points out that in "stronger" houses the multiple family groups could all be members of a larger kin group who shared common rights to resources passed down from a notable ancestor. Archaeological research supports this pattern in sites throughout the Lower Fraser Valley and Salish Sea regions. Long houses with multiple hearths appear at the DhRp52 site at ca. 4,500–5,000 years ago in the Pitt River area (Katzie Development Corporation 2014). Structure 3 at the Qithyil (Scowlitz) site dates to ca. 2000–2700 cal. BP and included multiple hearths indicative of several distinct families co-occupying the house (Lepofsky et al. 2009). Chatters (1989) documents large houses with multifamily spaces dating to the past 2,000 years at Tualdad Altu and Spabadid. Grier (2006) presents evidence for houses at Dionisio Point dating to ca. 1350–1400 cal. BP with four family hearths and a central hearth either for events or for use by a household chiefly family. In contrast, Stó:lō houses in sites located in the Lower Fraser Canyon (Sxwóxwiymelh, Welqámex, and Ts'qó:ls) near Hope, British Columbia, demonstrate consistent evidence for the use of central hearths. Lepofsky et al. (2009) suggest that houses could have been occupied by single or multiple families and that occupants likely slept around the periphery of the structure. Thus, these houses were likely organized more mutualistically, but it is unclear if they represented Houses in the sense of Lévi-Strauss (1982).

The best example of South Coast collectivist houses comes from the Chinookan groups of the Lower Columbia. Winter houses with open plans were organized with linear arrangements of family hearths down the center of the house, with cache pits placed on either side (Smith 2006). Other winter houses were organized in compartments that sheltered one or more families each (Ames and Sobel 2013). Spatial positioning of family living spaces in Chinookan houses reflected social standing such that high-status families resided in the rear and others closer to the front (Ames and Sobel 2013). Archaeological research at the Meier and Cathlapotl sites indicates that individual families engaged in the complete repertoire of domestic tasks (Ames and Sobel 2013), thus fitting the model of collectivist households. Other South Coast groups maintained similar multifamily houses. The Netarts Sand Spit site is an ancestral Tillamook village that contains long houses with centrally placed hearths and ovens (Newman 1959), likely representing spaces for families. Seaburg and Miller (1990) note that two families could share a common hearth, with sleeping platforms located on opposite sides and families also separated by partitions.

Groups from the North Coast organized themselves in hierarchically structured societies with Houses managed by a noble or chiefly class (Coupland et al. 2009). Lower-ranked commoners and slaves worked for the House but did not otherwise have rights. Thus, in essence, they acted as servants to the elite class. Mobility was highly constrained for titled members though commoners had more freedom to move between Houses. Houses were designed to reflect social ranking but work was organized communally. Thus, typical North Coast House groups conducted their work around a central hearth while families slept and stored their possessions in arrangements that included spaces for the house chief and family at the rear of the house, nobles on the lateral sides, and commoners and slaves near the entrance (Coupland et al. 2009). De Laguna (1972, 1990) describes Tlingit houses having a semi-subterranean central portion with a hearth surrounded by one or more raised wooden platforms on which the house members resided and stored their belongings (Figure 8). As was typical of North Coast groups, the chief resided at the back while other House members had space on the sides. Slaves slept at the entrance near where a variety of items including fresh water, game, urinals, and gear were kept. De Laguna et al. (1964)

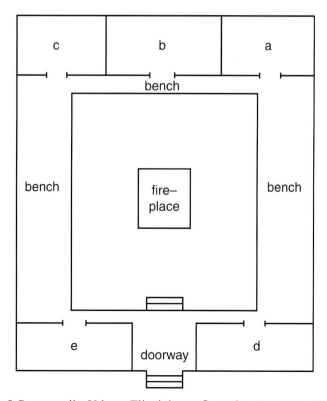

Figure 8 Communalist Yakutat Tlingit house floor plan (de Laguna 1972: 301).

provide archaeological evidence for this pattern from the Old Town site at Yakutat Bay. The Haida maintained similar houses to Tlingit groups. The largest and wealthiest houses could have multiple tiers occupied by families and individuals of different ranks (Blackman 1990; Swanton 1905). Slaves lived on the lowest level, persons of intermediate rank on middle levels, and chiefly families on the highest level, also positioned at the rear of the house. Fladmark (1973) and Acheson (1991) document this pattern in the archaeological record respectively at Richardson Ranch and Tc!u'uga. Tsimshian houses were organized in a similar fashion, with central hearths and distinct residential areas for nobles, commoners, and slaves. Archaeological evidence for Tsimshian houses is particularly good and derives from several sites. MacDonald and Cybulski (2001) document a central hearth in a historic period house at the Kitandach site. House O at McNichol Creek also contained a central hearth surrounded by sleeping platforms and dated ca. 1,600 years ago (Coupland 2006). There is some evidence that much older houses may have been more collectivist in organization, as suggested by the pair of hearths at the approximately 3,000-year-old Paul Mason site (Coupland 1985).

Wakashan-speaking groups relied upon an intermediate household strategy. While descent in North Coast groups was matrilineal, Wakashan groups were bilateral, which created the opportunity for greater individual mobility for House members (Coupland et al. 2009; Drucker 1951; Suttles 1968). Yet Wakashan Houses (Figure 9) were still tightly managed by chiefly groups much like those of the North Coast. Drucker's (1951) account of the Nuu-chah-nulth is particularly

Figure 9 Kwakwaka'wakw (Nimpkish) house front with images of thunderbird and orca (Boas 1897: 378).

instructive. While Nuu-chah-nulth residences were generally considered patri-local, there was in actuality no hard and fast rule. Thus, even chiefs could spend significant amounts of time away living with kin in other villages. Then there were two classes of lower-ranked people, those who were generally closely related to the chief and who resided in the house corners and others who were less well-connected and who lived in between the corners. The former received some privileges that helped bind them to the chief while the latter did not. Consequently, while both groups had the option to move, the latter were particularly mobile, to the point that they were termed "tenants" by Drucker (1951: 279) who notes that there was a "continual stream of people, mostly of low rank, pouring in and out of the houses." Thus, people would stay in one House for a time but periodically move on in order to not make relatives in other Houses jealous. While in a given House, however, each tenant provided complete loyalty, working exclusively for the good of that group. The frequency of individual mobility between Houses was not advantageous to chiefs, since even though a chief might hold rights to potentially lucrative resources, he also needed labor from House members to gain actual benefits. Consequently, smart chiefs worked to attract tenants with generosity and frequent feasts. Drucker (1951: 71) describes the spatial arrangements of Nuu-chah-nulth houses in some detail, noting that residence spaces of the chiefly and tenant-class families each included an individual fireplace, sleeping spaces, and storage areas. Activity areas surrounded the hearths and led to accumulated kitchen debris in these areas.

McMillan and Ste. Claire (2012) report on excavations of a large Nuu-chah-nulth house at the Huu7ii site on Barkley Sound that provide archaeological support for Drucker's (1951) descriptions. House 1 at the site contained a large centrally placed hearth feature and smaller such features closer to the walls of the house. McMillan and Ste. Claire (2012) interpret these respectively as feasting and family hearths, in line with Drucker's ethnography. The Makah people of northwestern Washington organized themselves in House groups similarly to the Nuu-chah-nulth (Renker and Gunther 1990). The most stable social positions were House heads (chiefs) and slaves. The middle group had more mobility options and could enhance or lose social standing depending upon marriages. Archaeological evidence from the Ozette site provides material details regarding Makah household organization (Samuels 2006). Distinctions in site spatial context, size, and internal arrangements of features and artifacts suggest that Houses were ranked – House 1 the highest and Houses 2 and 5 lesser. Each house then contains hearth features parallel to bench zones and walls indicating occupations by six to eight families. Finally, House 1 also contains a large hearth placed centrally on the floor, raising the possibility that it was used for elite feasting purposes.

3 Institutional Economy

The economies of Pacific Northwest societies were clearly managed at family and household levels. However, there is also tremendous diversity in wider institutional economies or the systems of production and consumption created by human organizations. In the Indigenous Pacific Northwest, these would have been what Hirth (2020: 43) terms "informal economic institutions" or, effectively, the range of strategic organizational strategies operated by cooperating households to their mutual benefit in meeting mutual biological and social needs. There is institutional variation in three specific areas: social groups (e.g. clans), political organizations, and secret societies. Activities of organizations within each of these affected the production, storage, and movement of goods. Economic decisions were made across multiple scales, spanning the decisions of family members to those of house and village heads and at times polity chiefs (often with associated councils). However, it is also clear that house, village, and polity heads rarely had coercive power and thus collective action was often predicated on chiefly oratory skills and acceptance by requisite groups (Ames 1995). I introduce institutional economies using three broad groupings: autonomous villages without clans; autonomous villages with clans; and local groups, tribes, confederacies, and chiefdoms (Figure 10). I follow with a short consideration of secret societies (Figure 11).

3.1 Autonomous Villages without Clans

I begin with variation in these groups starting with a consideration of those lacking clans or formal political units. As discussed, most Plateau groups did not maintain formal Houses and organized their economic production and exchange activities around meeting family needs. Yet ethnographers do describe the organization of bands and tribal divisions as having relatively flexible membership rules. The Coeur d'Alene people lacked clans and related societies, and individuals had substantial freedom to move between residential groups, which was a likely adaptive response to variation in resource conditions (Teit 1930). Coeur d'Alene bands were groups of related families who lived in a territorial landscape considered to be inherited from ancestors. Bands could unite into multi-band divisions during some seasons. Chiefs were elected and represented different levels, spanning local bands to divisions. Chiefs and councils made social and political decisions for their respective groups but do not appear to have otherwise controlled the production or distribution of resources beyond throwing feasts for the benefit of band members (Teit 1930). Okanagan and Sinixt groups lacked clans or societies, and like the Coeur d'Alene were organized in bands that held hereditary territory and sometimes aggregated into temporarily larger units

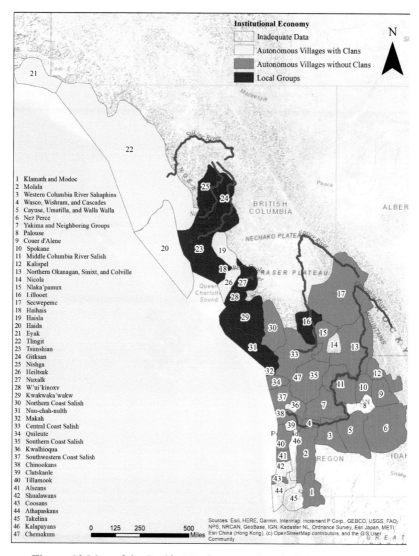

Figure 10 Map of the Pacific Northwest region depicting variation in Indigenous institutional strategies. Local groups refer to all of those who operated multi-village organizations of various scales, spanning local groups, tribes, confederacies, and chiefdoms.

(Teit 1930). Chiefs were hereditary when associated with bands but could also be elected for particular duties, including management during times of war and peace-making, hunting, and dancing. Other than hosting feasts and the sharing of accumulated goods, chiefs had no control over family economic production and distribution activities (Teit 1930). Secwepemc groups, with the exception of

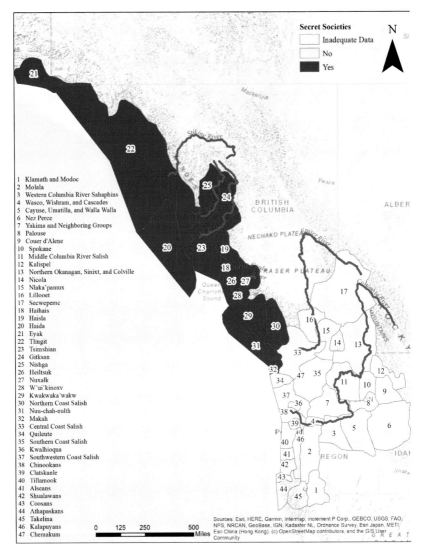

Figure 11 Map of the Pacific Northwest region depicting variation in Indigenous groups with and without secret societies.

the nineteenth-century Canyon Division, also lacked formal clans and were organized around bands who controlled communally owned territory (Teit 1909). Hereditary chiefs presided over bands while elected chiefs managed war, hunting, and dancing. As noted by Teit (1909: 570), chiefs did not maintain any special rights or opportunities beyond other band members. Rather, they provided wise counsel and demonstrated generosity through feasts and gifting. According to Ray (1933), Sanpoil groups were organized around autonomous villages made up of multiple families residing in winter homes. Ray does not mention clans or societies and notes that village membership was in constant flux as people moved in and out, thus resembling the Okanagan and Sinixt bands described by Teit (1930). Sanpoil village chiefs were hereditary, though village members could vote for a preferred individual when more than one person was eligible. There were also subchiefs who were effectively assistants to the chief, but there were no elected chiefs for particular activities. As with other Plateau groups, chiefs carried little economic authority but remained influential if they were generous with their wealth (Ray 1933). The Wenatchi and other Mid-Columbia Salishan groups appear to have been organized in a very similar fashion (Miller 1998).

Other major groups lacking clans were the Salishan- and Chinookan-speaking communities of the Central and South Coast. Differing from the Plateau examples, these groups did organize themselves in House groups with hereditarily ranked extended families. Stó:lō groups organized themselves in autonomous villages and in some areas more complex political configurations (Duff 1952). Stó:lō leadership was based upon hereditary heads of extended family groups usually residing together within houses of various sizes. Those of the highest rank could be considered leaders of entire villages. Family heads could not coerce economic activities, yet they remained highly influential within their family units and in some cases beyond. Thus, they could help family members with the arrangement of marriages and organize feasts and potlatches to relieve debt and maintain social status (Duff 1952). Central Coast Salish groups (e.g. Squamish, Cowichan, and Sechelt) were organized in a similar manner. Barnett (1955) notes that while headman was an inherited position, individuals had to work to maintain a following. This was accomplished through a range of different attributes and strategies. Headmen provided advice and counsel, though they could not enforce their will upon their House groups. They typically were entitled to returns on fishing, hunting, and gathering but were also generous with goods and put on feasts for family groups and outside groups whenever possible. The latter events were more lavish and required a longer period of investment to be fully prepared.

The Southwest Coast communities also lacked clans, though some ethnographers speculate that clans may have existed in the more ancient past (e.g. Powell and Jensen 1976). The Quinault organized themselves in autonomous villages made up of Houses, each with an "owner," though according to Olson (1936) this was different from the household chiefs or headmen of groups to the north in the sense that owners were better understood as partners within their household groups. Yet Olson (1936) does describe a Quinault village chief, a hereditary position belonging to the owner of the highest-ranked House in each village. Village chiefs caried no formal authority yet were highly influential. They also maintained certain economic rights (e.g. ownership of the best fishing site) and were expected to be generous by sponsoring periodic feasts and potlatches. Chinookan groups organized in villages and local groups consisting of kin-based networks of house groups (Hajda 2013). House groups included as few as one and as many as fourteen nuclear family groups and were managed by a household head chosen by a combination of hereditary and earned status. This household leader appears to have been largely responsible for managing food production and distribution, providing advice, and settling issues between household members. Household heads gained influence that was recognized across village to multi-village networks by their demonstrated ability to amass wealth, gain followers (through wisdom and generosity), and establish social contacts, presumably for marriages and exchange purposes. However, like many other Central and South Coast groups, even the highest-ranked household heads (in effect, village chiefs) carried no ability to use coercive authority in economic ventures (Hajda 2013).

3.2 Autonomous Villages with Clans

A number of North Coast groups maintained autonomous villages yet also organized their socio-economic lives around powerful clans. Tlingit house groups (communalist Houses) were occupied and managed by male kin of the same matrilineal lineage, clan, and moiety (de Laguna 1990; "moieties" are also called "phratries" by Oberg 1973). Thus, house groups were made up of brothers, sons of brothers' sisters, and sons of the daughters of those sisters. Wives were always of a different clan or moiety. The oldest male was house chief, who served as ceremonial leader, advisor, educator, and keeper of stories and other knowledge. He did not lead war or economic activities and was replaced by the next oldest brother after death. Major economic activities spanning subsistence production, feasting, potlatching, and raiding were organized by the house group. House property, including ceremonial items, large canoes, slaves, major weapons, and utensils, was generally transmitted between generations within the House. Other property could be used for the purposes of exchange and bridge gifts. Oberg (1973: 38) defines the Tlingit clan as "a group of individuals living in a number of villages who identify themselves using a common name, a number of crests, and who believe in a common local origin." In practicality, this meant a group related on the female line practicing exogamy. Clan membership was important at two scales. The whole clan rarely acted as a unit, though it was possible in times of major feuds or war. Local divisions of clans were more important as each owned rights to hunting and fishing areas and village spaces where houses could be built. House groups owned patches on the landscape known to have abundant herbs, roots, berries, and useful tree species. The clan also played a significant role in organizing major potlatches, as when a house group proposed to organize such an event permission from other house groups within the clan division was required. It was also understood that, upon a return, potlatch-received goods would be redistributed (Oberg 1973). The Tlingit moieties (Raven, Wolf, and Eagle) did not act as socio-economic units but rather provided guidance for marriages and ritual procedures along with providing labor for ceremonies. Thus, in essence, membership in moieties provided Tlingit people with a certain degree of "psychic unity," given that all members claimed a common origin and certain embodied characteristics (e.g. warlike, wise, etc.) (Oberg 1973: 48).

Haida socio-political organization had both similarities to and differences from their neighbors, the Tlingit. Haida people identified two moieties (Eagle and Raven), within which existed multiple matrilineal subgroups variously termed "families" (Swanton 1905), "clans" (Murdock 1934), and "lineages" (Blackman 1990; Drucker 1955). The latter groups were made up of individual house groups or communalist Houses. Lineages/clans were social groups who claimed a common ancestry recorded in mythical stories (Swanton 1905). Lineage/clan groups had socio-economic power in their ability to control access to both corporeal and noncorporeal property, much like those of the Tlingit. They controlled rights to vegetative patches, lakes, salmon streams, trapping locales, and house sites within winter villages. They also controlled rights to names and crests (lineage/clan symbols) (Blackman 1990; Swanton 1905). Hereditary chiefs with considerable authority were central to the activities of lineages/clans and were recognized on three levels (Blackman 1990; Swanton 1905). House or "sub-lineage" chiefs had authority over members of the house group and could decide on economic issues like movement to fish camps as well as putting together groups to wage war. Lineage/clan chiefs had to be consulted regarding the use of lineage/clan resources and property as well as a range of other matters, including warfare. Finally, in Haida settlements (Figure 12) with more than one lineage/clan, the highest-ranking (most wealthy and influential) lineage/clan chief (of the lineage/clan owning the settlement site) served as "town mother" or "town master" and held wide authority (Swanton 1905). Inheritance of chiefly positions was based upon seniority within the Haida matrilineal system such that titles went to brothers in order of age or the eldest son of the eldest sister (Blackman 1990).

The Haisla people spoke a variant of Wakashan similar to Kwakwaka'wakw groups to the south. Yet their socio-political organization was much closer to other North Coast groups, especially the neighboring Tsimshian (Hamori-Torok 1990). While the Haisla were organized geographically in two divisions with

Figure 12 The Haida village, Skidegate (Swanton 1905: plate X).

major winter villages at Kitlope and Kitimaat (Drucker 1955), these groups do not appear to have wielded socio-economic power. Rather, Haisla village groups were organized socially around six matrilineal clans: Beaver, Blackfish (Orca), Crow, Eagle, Raven, and Salmon. While clans were independent, they also formed alliances that affected marriage arrangements and structured potlatch and feast events (Olson 1940). Lineages within each clan maintained a variety of properties, including land, houses, and fishing grounds. They also owned noncorporeal property, including names, songs, dances, and ceremonies (Drucker 1955). Like other Northwest Coast groups, society was also divided into three groups: nobles (titled people), commoners (untitled people), and slaves. Nobles could enter chiefly position at the levels of lineages and clans. Lineage chiefs were active managers of corporeal and noncorporeal property and thus controlled group movements to and from fishing sites, bestowed names in naming ceremonies, and made decisions as to appropriate crests displayed and songs sung in ceremonial events. Effective decision-making on the part of chiefs had significant down-the-line impacts on the long-term viability and standing of their associated social groups (Drucker 1955).

3.3 Local Groups, Tribes, Confederacies, and Chiefdoms

As noted by Drucker (1955), a number of Northwest Coast groups developed and operated multi-village political units with a high degree of variation. Here, I draw on descriptions and associated terminology from the ethnographic and archaeological literature to explore variability in the structure of political relationships and centralized authority with its economic implications. I begin with local groups and tribes and follow with confederacies and, finally, potential examples of chiefdoms.

Kwakwaka'wakw groups were organized on three levels (collectivist houses, social groups, and tribes). Named houses were ranked members of social groups termed "numayms" by Boas (1966). Numaym groups appear to have provided the fundamental inspiration for Lévi-Strauss' (1982) concept of Houses.

As noted by Codere (1990), numayms were powerful organizations that maintained ownership and control of corporeal and noncorporeal property. Thus, they owned house sites and food resource procurement localities along with rights to titles and crests and all of their signifiers as depicted on poles (often colloquially termed "totem poles"), house fronts, house posts, and feasting dishes. Further, they controlled songs, ceremonies, and names. Titles and names were of central importance within the placing of individuals during the ceremonies associated with potlatches. Since Kwakwaka'wakw descent was bilateral, individuals could in theory be members of multiple numayms (Rosman and Rubel 1971). Yet membership was complicated by the fact that numayms were ranked and held only a limited number of membership seats. Thus, activation of membership depended upon age such that the eldest child within a given family was assigned to a seat in a higher-ranked numaym and younger children to lesser seats. This made for competition between siblings that was often replicated across generations (Rosman and Rubel 1971). Village leadership included extended family (generally House) chiefs who were custodians of rights regarding access to food resources and ownership and management of family property. Numayms were also managed by chiefs who were ranked in alignment with their numaym status (Rosman and Rubel 1971). Kwakwaka'wakw people were also organized socio-politically in what Boas (1966) termed "tribes," each containing several numaym groups (Rosman and Rubel 1971) and managed by a hierarchy of chiefs drawn from those groups (Drucker 1955). Codere (1990) notes that there were approximately thirty such tribal groups who held a particular territory within which was located a major winter village and a series of smaller seasonal villages and camps. Codere (1990) also notes that intertribal relationships were not stable prior to about 1900 CE when potlatching systems united all into a single system of alliances and rankings. Prior to this time, local alliances were established for the purposes of marriages, defense, and potlatching (Drucker 1955; Rosman and Rubel 1971).

Drucker (1951) describes four scales of northern Nuu-chah-nulth sociopolitical organization. Collectivist House groups formed the basis of society and were made up of noble and commoner families. Drucker notes that the typical House held four ranked chiefs who were typically closely related kin (often brothers). The highest-ranked House chief was considered the owner of the house itself, while the lesser chiefs owned their residential positions within the house. Houses (one or more) also represented local groups, which owned territory and ritual and ceremonial property (Kenyon 1980). Local groups could be subdivided into individual lineage groups (with their own Houses) representing distinct founding ancestors, and the senior lineage head was considered head chief of the local group. Local groups were not normally autonomous amongst the northern Nuu-chah-nulth and were thus typically aligned with several others sharing a single large winter village with a prescribed hierarchy of chiefs and material status indicators, including substantial houses and named carved posts. These "tribal" groups could also be aligned with several other such groups as "confederacies" who provided political and cultural solidarity to all members and could organize warfare and major ceremonial events (Drucker 1951: 220–221). The members of confederacies met at a common summer village, facilitating collective offshore fishing and hunting along with a reification of chiefly ranking as expressed in ritual seating during ceremonies. These confederacies represented the major divisions of the northern Nuu-chah-nulth, for example the Kyoquot, Ehetisat, Nuchatlet, and Moachat groups (Drucker 1951: 221). In contrast, McMillan and St. Claire (2012) argue that southern Nuu-chah-nulth groups were often quite different. They note that autonomous local groups occupied territories in the Barkley Sound area at a higher density than groups in the north. They also argue that four local groups amalgamated into a more complex political entity ancestral to the Huu-ay-aht Nuu-chah-nulth immediately prior to European contact. The new political entity, resembling a tribe in Drucker's (1951) terms, managed a larger territory, which allowed a higher degree of flexibility to member groups regarding land use and resource procurement (McMillan and St. Claire 2012).

The Upper Lillooet or St'át'imc of the western Canadian Plateau also operated a multitiered socio-political system, though one that was different from the Nuu-chah-nulth or Kwakwaka'wakw. Like those groups, the fundamental political unit was the House group, consisting of several families residing together in one house (generally collectivist) or in multiple smaller residences (Prentiss and Kuijt 2012). House groups were members of clans led by a hereditary chief (Kennedy and Bouchard 1998a; Teit 1906). When a village held multiple clans, the hereditary chief of the founding clan was also the village chief. If a clan extended to multiple villages, one chief would still preside over the activities of the clan (Teit 1906). Clan chiefs held no special privileges over other members yet were trusted to make critical decisions regarding the scheduling of economically important activities and the use of lands owned by the clan. Thus, in effect, the clans controlled the access and use of fishing locales, hunting lands, and plant patches. The fact of multiple clans spread across multiple villages meant that the landscape was divided into a collage of jurisdictions (Prentiss et al. in press). This meant that ease of access to clan-owned resources must have varied substantially, leading to some degree of material wealth-based distinctions between clan groups within the villages. The ability to amass wealth and to demonstrate generosity through potlatching also meant that wealth-based social distinctions and achieved chiefly status were also possible within the clans (Prentiss et al. in press; Kennedy and Bouchard 1998a). Prentiss et al. (in press) term these geographically overlapping groups "clan-based confederacies" and argue that this situation would have thus reflected the operation of both heterarchical and hierarchical power structures within St'át'imc communities.

The Lower Fraser Canyon Stó:lō are considered members of the wider Central Coast Salish group and as such have long been thought to have been primarily organized from a political standpoint in autonomous villages (Matson and Coupland 1995; Mitchell 1983). However, scholars have periodically argued that some Coast Salish group political organizations spanned multiple villages (e.g. Tollefson 1987). Schaepe (2006) offers a compelling argument that the Fraser Canyon Stó:lō developed a multitiered political strategy resembling a chiefdom. He begins by arguing that Miller's (1998) "corporate family group" model is a useful construct for understanding within and between-group relationships in the Lower Fraser Canyon. Rather than seeing families within villages as entirely autonomous units, Miller's scenario views them as working in cooperative networks. Labor is thus developed and organized by leaders to maximize production, whether in subsistence activities like fishing or architectural construction (Schaepe 2006). Schaepe (2006: 699) suggests that we view networked cooperating groups more as a social fabric upon which new forms of cooperation are derived. Under conditions of severe raiding by other groups, the corporate family group model would have provided a framework for establishing inter-village cooperation to construct and maintain defensive networks. Oral histories suggest that a specific "head man" identified as *Liquitem* was "boss of the whole river," controlling the operations of multiple chiefs and including the ability to conscript entire villages to fight when needed (Schaepe 2006: 700). This implies that these communities recognized central leadership that had the power to control nonkin labor, a hallmark of chiefdom-like organization (Arnold 1993). Thus, the Lower Fraser Canyon Stó:lō organized a system that incorporated leadership spanning family, village, and multi-village levels that was most fully integrated when developing defenses against annual raids from other groups. It is less clear how such a political organization impacted other economic strategies associated with goods production and exchange.

The Tsimshian groups inclusive of the Nishga, Gitksan, and Tsimshian proper were organized in a complex system of family lineages, clans, subclans and Houses, local groups, and, at least briefly, a regional polity (Garfield 1939). The Tsimshian divided themselves into four matrilineal exogamous clans – Eagle, Raven, Wolf, and Blackfish (orca) – with each represented by crests owned by their respective groups. Clans were, in turn, divided into subclans, with membership based upon inherited stories confirming common origin. Subclans were further divided into descent groups termed "Houses" (Garfield 1939: 174). Any given House was made up of one or more matriline lineages and owned rights to socio-economic privileges, names, crests, stories, songs, and dances along with territories for fishing, hunting, and berry gathering (Garfield 1939). Villages were made up of sets of house properties (organized internally with communalist strategies) representing House groups, and sets of geographically proximate villages could be established via a fission of Houses thus forming local groups or what Garfield (1939: 175) calls "tribes." Amongst Tsimshian and Nishga groups, chiefs were ranked by House such that village chief represented the highest-ranked House and had authority over the others (Garfield 1939; Halpin and Seguin 1990). Chiefs received substantial economic support from their communities in the way of tribute often paid in the form of food. Yet chiefs were also expected to provide for their people, whether in the form of good decision-making or the offering of their food stores by various means, including frequent feasting events (Garfield 1939).

Martindale (2003) presents evidence from a variety of historical, ethno-logical, and archaeological sources to suggest that a Tsimshian paramount chiefdom was established during the early to middle nineteenth century CE. In brief, he recognizes a nested hierarchy of political groups that include lineage groups organized on the basis of descent rules and village groups organized by rank as associated with inherited and achieved positions. He argues that a third level in the hierarchy is recognizable in the establishment of chiefly positions presiding over the village chiefs. Evidence suggests that a Tsimshian village chief, *Ligeex*, took advantage of changes brought by the European fur trade demands. Using his network of alliances, *Ligeex* came to control the entire Metlakhatla Tsimshian area, thus favoring regional political authority, expanded economic control over goods production and exchange, and extreme differentiation in material wealth (Martindale 2003: 48). While this system was short-lived, it illustrates the potential for individuals and associated factions to gain significant economic and political power by careful social maneuvering.

3.4 Secret Societies

Secret societies were essential to the socio-economic and political structure of many Northwest Coast groups. Hayden (2018) suggests that a secret society is best defined "as an association with internal ranks in which membership especially in the upper ranks, is exclusive, voluntary, and associated with secret knowledge" (Johansen 2004: 10; cited in Hayden 2018). Scholars have disagreed over the role of secret societies, leading to debate between those who favor such groups engaged in building social unity (Levy 1992) versus a counter perspective that they formed to help control the production and distribution of material resources (Hayden 2018). Northwest Coast ethnographers have generally confirmed that latter position, noting that secret societies were organizations dedicated to establishing and reinforcing the desires of elite segments of society (Boas 1897; Drucker 1941). This does not necessarily mean that rituals (and associated artistic imagery) performed by secret society members did not also reinforce prevailing beliefs about the nature of society and the world around them. I recognize a number of economic aspects to the operation of secret societies on the Northwest Coast. First, there could be significant costs for gaining membership and rising in leadership hierarchies. As noted by Drucker (1941; see also Hayden 2018), such fees included hosting significant potlatches and feasts. Second, secret societies reinforced their power with dramatic and costly performances that included the display of dramatic costumes (Figure 13) in social events (e.g. dances), destruction of wealth, creation of illusions, and killing of slaves (Hayden 2018). Third, activities of secret societies were often designed to reinforce rights of noble and chiefly elites to corporeal and non-corporeal property (Codere 1950; Drucker 1941; Spradley 1969). Fourth, punishments for those who broke secret society rules could be severe and included death in some cases (Boas 1897; McIlwraith 1948).

Secret societies existed in nearly all groups from the Central and Northern Coasts. All were similar in their basic structural characteristics, though there was also variation in ideological and practical details (Hayden 2018; Loeb 1929). Olson (1936) describes two secret societies amongst the Quinault, identified as tsa'djak and klo'kwalle. The latter was typical of power-associated secret societies with a membership of wealthy males, while the former was a curing society whose membership was largely female. The Nuu-chah-nulth held an annual "shaman's dance" organized and managed by the elite "wolf societies," in which initiates who had been "captured" by supernatural wolves and other spirits were ritually purified (Drucker 1951: 386). Drucker (1951: 217) also describes a healing society with an associated ritual known as *tsaiyeq*. The Central Coast Salish included a secret society associated

Figure 13 Kwakwaka'wakw Hamatsa raven mask (Boas 1897: 447).

with spirit possession dances (Barnett 1955). The Hamatsa and associated societies of the Kwakwaka'wakw organized complex winter ceremonials in which initiates were transformed back from a state of spirit possession to an acceptable state of humanity (Boas 1897, 1966). The *Sisauk* society was an elite organization in Nuxalk communities that also held elaborate dances associated with the transformation of initiates (McIlwraith 1948). The Dog Eater and Dancer societies organized the complex Tsimshian ceremonies known as *t'sik* and *sem-hala'it*, both associated with the establishment of spirit power in young initiates (Garfield 1939). The Haida had multiple secret societies charged with performing dances during potlatches, some of which include the ritual transformations of spirit-possessed initiates (Swanton 1905). De Laguna (1972) notes that secret societies in southern Tlingit groups organized performances and stunts but that such societies were not known for the Yakutat Tlingit.

4 Specialization

Craft specialization has been widely recognized as an essential element of Indigenous cultures of the Pacific Northwest (e.g. Drucker 1955, 1965). Consequently, there has been considerable discussion of the variable role of specialists in reproducing Northwest Coast beliefs and maintaining domestic and institutional economies (e.g. Ames 1995; Brumfiel and Earle 1987; Costin 1991; Hayden 1995, 2014; Hirth 2020). Ames (1995: 158) introduces the concept of embedded specialists for the Northwest Coast, noting that specialization in the production of goods was typically accomplished by skilled craftspeople often drawn from the elite or noble (title-holding) stratum of society and who were neither contractually obligated nor producing for a "demand crowd." It is most critical to realize that embedded specialists were members of Houses and consequently service to those groups was their primary occupation. Thus, their craft production work was not necessarily full-time, as seasonally they could also be in demand for aid in basic subsistence and related activities. This contrasts with other noninstitutionalized systems of craft production where producers were attached full-time in singular workshops and manufactories, sometimes performing work as members of guilds (Hirth 2020).

Labor specialization was part of a more complex system of labor allocation in Pacific Northwest societies. While gender clearly played a role in some critical aspects of labor (e.g. men generally fished for salmon and women did the processing), kinship was the primary basis for labor mobilization (Donald 1997). Elites (title-holders) could engage in labor (embedded specialists, for example), direct labor (i.e. chiefs making decisions regarding subsistence pursuits), and request labor from commoners, to which commoners would typically oblige given that title-holders controlled rights to resources. However, commoners also held the right not to cooperate if demands exceeded the potential for long-term payoffs. Mobilization of labor could be a significant challenge if demands were extreme and commoner relationships by kin limited. Building a kin base required time for reproduction, and some Houses could be challenged for adequate numbers of workers during periods of demographic stress (Ames 2006). Thus, slave labor was an important option (Donald 1997). Slaves as nonhuman beings could work outside the normal sexual division of labor and thus could engage in any production activity (Ames 1995). Slaves were obtained through birth, inheritance, payments, gifts, raiding, and exchange and served to help with a wide range of tasks including collecting firewood, collecting bark and other forest products, building shelters, helping with fishing, repairing houses, aiding in canoe manufacture, and acting as personal attendants (Donald 1997: 127). Slaves also played roles in select ceremonies, worked as guards, and participated in warfare and assassinations (Donald 1997: 128). Slaves were thus not craft specialists but could serve as aids to those persons.

Truly specialist production required the actions of highly trained craftspeople. Ames (1995) notes that such individuals were often title-holders who worked within their own Houses but who could also be hired by others. Thus, there were specialists in woodworking as required for canoes, poles, houses, masks, and serving bowls (Ames 1995). Others specialized in work with stone (e.g. Darwent 1998; Morin 2015), basketry (e.g. Turner 1998, 2014), and weavings from dog and mountain goat hair (Barsh et al. 2006). Men and women clearly contributed to specialist production efforts. The production of goods in the Pacific Northwest was critical for maintaining the status of the House and its membership. Goods were central to the maintenance of exchange relations and participation in potlatching networks. Ultimately, they served as a tool to maintain House membership and to attract and retain new members, an essential requirement for the viability of the House in the long term (Ames 1995, 2006). Because craft specialization in the Pacific Northwest was embedded into a complex system of status marking, ritual generosity, exchange relations, and, ultimately, maintenance of House populations, craft specialists did not suffer the same "craftsperson's dilemma" (Hirth 2020: 244) as crafters of other societies more dependent upon markets. Higher numbers of specialists tend to be associated with higher-density populations with more intensive ritual demands (Figure 14).

Tlingit, Tsimshian, and Haida maintained dense permanent villages with multiple specialists. These groups maintained production activities with many similarities, though the published literature is inconsistent on details. Oberg (1973) notes that Tlingit specialists could be retained to manufacture a variety of goods through a gifting process such that lower-valued items such as harpoons and cooking boxes (and presumably a wider range of items that could include basketry, fur/hide clothing, bark hats, and fishing gear) would require only a single gift. However, more valued items such as canoes (Figure 15), shell ornaments, and ceremonial robes (e.g. Chilkat blankets) might require multiple gifts. House building and pole carving (Figure 16) were ritualized activities organized and carried out by the opposite moiety such that workers were rewarded with gifts and a feast (Oberg 1973). Indeed, woodworking and painting were particularly important specializations on the North Coast, thus providing a good example of Ames' (1995) concept of embedded specialists. Woodcarving among the coastal Tsimshian was largely an elite status specialty that had its own social group identified as *gitsonket* who produced masks and house screens and even provided chiefly counsel (Ames 1995). Such individuals could be commissioned to create new works but did not depend on clients and as such were able to move on to other projects in other houses, communities, and even linguistic groups, as per Ames' (1995: 175) example of Tsimshian carvers who created the Yakutat Tlingit "rain screen" in the town of Klukwan. Haida carvers also specialized in the production of argillite sculptures as demand increased during the Colonial period (Swanton 1905).

Codere (1950, 1990; see also Boas 1911–1914) offers some details on Kwakwaka'wakw general and specialist production. A substantial quantity of household goods production was oriented towards routine subsistence technologies. Major items included canoes and boat-related parts, bags, baskets,

Figure 14 Map of the Pacific Northwest region depicting variation in Indigenous occupational specialists (for data and discussion, see Binford 2001).

tumplines, digging sticks, spades, fishing tackle including hooks of various sizes, racks, mats, weapons (spears), and clothing. House specialists also made particularly fine examples of wooden boxes, mats, bark and fur blankets, horn spoons, wooden dishes, and canoes that could be used in the potlatch (Codere 1950). Woodworking specialists were employed in the manufacture of poles, house posts, and wall planks (Codere 1990). Despite the wide array of specialty crafts, there were no full-time craft specialists (Codere 1990). Drucker (1951)

PIROGUE DU PORT DES FRANÇAIS.

Figure 15 Yakutat Tlingit canoe (de Laguna 1972: 954).

provides considerable detail regarding Nuu-chah-nulth crafting. Skilled carpenters played a significant role in the production and assembly of the large winter houses, a process that included the carving of house posts. A second specialist craft was canoe-making, a complex process involving the choice of wood, shaping and hollowing, and finishing. Multiple canoe forms were created, including those for freight, whaling, fur seal hunting, fishing, and small "rough" canoes used for collecting shellfish, children's play, and other activities (Drucker 1951: 84). Dentalium shell beads were a final specialist item that were mass-produced for local use and exchange purposes. As noted by Drucker (1951: 111), the Nuu-chah-nulth were the only group to have actual dentalium beds available offshore. Beyond specialist items, Nuu-chah-nulth crafters manufactured a wide range of wooden boxes, utensils, textiles, clothing and ornaments, tumplines, musical instruments, and blankets (Drucker 1951). The Ozette site, in the Makah area of northwest Washington State, provides archaeological support for social distinctions in goods production. Prentiss, Foor, and Murphy (2018) demonstrate significant variation at the site in wealth items (classified as wooden boxes and decorated items) between houses that is not replicated in other utilitarian gear (e.g. fishing gear, land hunting tools, and woodworking tools).

Figure 16 Haida crest ("totem") pole (Swanton 1905: 128).

A substantial number of additional groups normally occupying smaller villages also maintained high numbers of specialists. These groups are scattered across the Central, South, and Southwest Coast Salish, Lower Columbia, and Oregon Coast areas. The Squamish produced a wide variety of standard utilitarian and specialist goods (Barnett 1955). Major items included reef nets and seines, basketry traps, various hand nets, seal nets, goat snares, beaver harpoons, canoes including "shovel-nosed" varieties, weavings on roller looms, and cedar bark bags. Specialist contributions focused on woodworking provided opportunities for achieved status and material gain for expert producers (Barnett 1955: 107). Woodworking contributions in the Squamish and wider Salish Sea area included utensils, weapons, canoes, paddles, boxes, and house planks. Canoe-making was of special importance and the skill was transmitted across generations thus maintaining this specialty within family lines (Barnett 1955: 110). Although they apparently did not carry supernatural significance, finely woven dog hair blankets were also a craft specialty amongst the Central Coast Salish, including the Squamish (Barnett 1955: 120). The Quinault and Quileute occupied adjacent landscapes in coastal western Washington State and had similar traditions regarding specialist goods production (Olson 1936; Powell 1990; Powell and Jensen 1976). Olson (1936) notes that Quinault specialists exchanged services in return for other goods and services. There were a range of specialists, with house plank manufacture, canoe-making, and basket production being good examples (Olson 1936: 94). Thus, as elsewhere on the Coast, woodworking was especially highly regarded. Multiple forms of canoes and associated paddles were created, including ocean or whaling, sealing, river, small river or "ducking," and sea otter (Olson 1936: 67). Designs were similar to those of the Nuu-chah-nulth, their neighbors to the north. Other wooden items of importance included boat bailers, bows, arrows, boxes, platters or trays, and various utensils. Dog hair blankets similar to those of the Central Coast Salish were made, as were a variety of baskets, cord, mats, and nets (Olson 1936).

Chinookan households produced a vast array of items, including dentalium shell, obsidian products, canoes, boxes, bowls, figurines, hides, utensils, and baskets (Ames and Sobel 2013; Hajda and Sobel 2013; Silverstein 1990). Ames and Sobel (2013: 141–142) note that there were no full-time craft specialists in Chinookan households and that "everybody did everything." However, it is also clear that within Houses select family groups emphasized certain production efforts over others. This may have included the production of copper items, hides, and select wood and horn utensils (Ames and Sobel 2013; Silverstein 1990). There appears to be less understanding of how this form of embedded specialist production was integrated into household economies as related to social obligations and the exchange of goods (Ames and Sobel 2013). Chinookan villages were typically major trade centers.

Some Coastal and many Plateau groups resided in small seasonal villages and had few or no identified craft specialists. Yet community members still produced a range of specialized craft goods. Similar to the Central Coast Salish (Barnett 1955), the Stó:lō also recognized woodworking as a critical craft. Stó:lō crafters created wooden planks, house posts, multiple canoe forms, paddles, bailers, weapons, snowshoes, dishes, and various utensils (Duff 1952). Other significant crafts included hide clothing, dog wool blankets, basketry, nets, rope, and stone pipes (Duff 1952). Economic factors underlying Stó:lō production were likely similar to those for other Central Coast Salish groups (Barnett 1955). Lillooet groups produced a variety of specialized products for internal use and exchange. Lower Lillooet (Lil'wat) households produced wood products, hides, and mountain goat wool blankets. Upper Lillooet (St'át'imc) manufactured bark products including hemp line and bark twine and rope, along with hides, copper sheets and ornaments, mountain goat wool blankets, and nephrite jade tools, especially adzes (Morin 2012; Teit 1906). All produced basketry, wooden utensils, and house furniture. While ethnographies do not directly speak to the household economics of specialist production, it is clear that select tasks (nephrite tools, wool blankets, copper products) required significant investment in time and effort to learn and engage with these skills (e.g. Darwent 1998). Returns on the production of specialist items included prestige from gifting and valued goods from exchange relationships. It is unlikely that embedded specialists were present in most other Plateau groups. However, all produced a limited range of goods used in gifting and exchange. Wenatchi, Coeur d'Alene, Sinixt, Okanagan, Sanpoil, Nlaka'pamux, and Secwepemc groups produced hide products including bags and clothing along with a range of woven items (baskets, mats, and bags), nets, stone items (ground stone hammers, pestles, figurines, and grinding slabs), bone beads, and bark products (Teit 1900, 1909, 1930).

5 Distribution

Indigenous societies of the Pacific Northwest region operated within complex webs of social relationships. Uneven distributions of natural resources favored the exchange of goods to support local domestic economies, a standard expectation of societies economically centered on House groups (Hirth 2020; Wilk and Netting 1984). As noted by Tushingham et al. (2021), fat and carbohydrates were critical elements for winter diets long on lean protein. Thus, surplus production and exchange of fats for eulachon and sea mammals along with berries and geophytes were essential for survival by groups throughout the region. Nonlocal raw material for goods manufacture was also essential for many groups and that could span hides for clothing, wood for canoes, and stone for a variety of tool forms. However, exchange relationships went far beyond minimal needs for domestic economies. The political economies of Pacific Northwest groups located on the Coast and western river valleys of the Interior also depended upon the acquisition of valued goods, including sheet copper, goat and spruce root blankets, furs, and shells for jewelry. These items were used for the display of status and in ritual generosity (e.g. potlatching) to ensure group social standing and advancement. At a deeper level, social negotiations also helped to maintain House membership and village stability (Ames 1995, 2006).

5.1 Exchange

It should be clear by now that Pacific Northwest socio-economies did not function solely at the scale of local groups of villages. Ames and Maschner (1999), drawing on Suttles (1990b) and Mitchell and Donald (1988), argue that the Northwest Coast region was subdivided into north and south regional networks within which goods and cultural traditions were widely shared (Figure 17). The north network includes the ethnographic Tlingit, Haida, and Tsimshian areas.

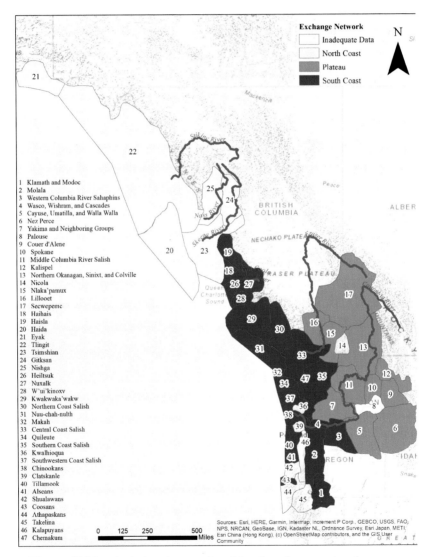

Figure 17 Map depicting three regional-level exchange networks among Indigenous groups of the Pacific Northwest.

The south network is subdivided into smaller groups focused in the Kwakwaka'wakw and Nuxálk, Nuu-chah-nulth/Makah, Central and Southern Coast Salish, Chinookan, and general Oregon and Northern California coast areas. Hayden and Schulting (1997) add a third network focused on the greater Plateau generally inclusive of the Fraser–Thompson and Columbia River drainages. Some ethnographers (e.g. Oberg 1973) have suggested that Indigenous Pacific Northwest groups in pre-Colonial times did not possess knowledge of true bartering systems, thus preferring gifting. Mitchell and Donald (1988) argue, however, that there is abundant evidence from around the region that Indigenous groups at first contact with Europeans were fully familiar with the concept of bartering and trade. As noted by Ames (1995), exchange was an essential component of Pacific Northwest socio-economies, as manifested at domestic and ritual levels on scales spanning households to wider social entities.

The North Coast exchange network incorporated the Tlingit, Haida, and Tsimshian, along with more distant trade partners on the Interior and further south on the Coast. Tlingit exchange was organized at House and clan levels, with the actual work of accumulating goods and engaging in sometimes lengthy trips managed by specialists termed *yitsati* (Oberg 1973: 105). Maintaining long-distance trade was dangerous yet considered socio-economically critical as nonlocal foods and goods were needed in all communities. It is not surprising that the most profitable trade routes into the Interior were actually owned by the most powerful Tlingit clans (Oberg 1973). Tlingit trade networks operated on three scales: Island and mainland Tlingit, Haida and Tsimshian, and Athabaskan and South Coast groups (Oberg 1973). Mainland Tlingit produced a wide range of hides and hide products, mountain goat and big horn sheep horn products, Chilkat blankets, and highly valued foods including dried eulachon, eulachon oil, and berries. Island Tlingit in return produced yew food, cedar bark and various associated products (e.g. watertight baskets), and green stone, along with foods including dried venison, seaweed, herring, halibut, and king (spring/Chinook) salmon, various shellfish, herring eggs, and seal oil. Tlingit groups greatly valued Interior Athabaskan goods that included hides (especially marmot skins) and hide products (many clothing items), along with sinew and hammered sheet copper (Figure 18). Coastal Tsimshian groups specialized in the production of high-quality eulachon oil, which was in demand in many communities including those of the Haida, Tlingit, Gitksan, and Heiltsuk (Garfield 1939; Mitchell and Donald 1988; Oberg 1973). Not surprisingly, the major Metlakhatla Tsimshian villages served as major trade centers. Tsimshian groups also traded horn spoons, seaweed, soap berries, and slaves (Halpin and Seguin 1990). Haida traders offered cedar canoes, shell items, dried halibut, and

Figure 18 Kwakwaka'wakw copper with hawk image (Boas 1897: 343).

slaves (Mitchell and Donald 1988; Oberg 1973). Tlingit traders exchanged Chilkat blankets, hides, and copper with these groups (Oberg 1973).

The South Coast exchange network was more realistically a collection of complex relationships with many local core areas (Ames and Maschner 1999; Suttles 1990c). Wakashan-speaking groups (Nuu-chah-nulth and Kwakwaka'wakw) shared a variety of cultural traits, fishing and sea mammal hunting gear, masks, and various ritual traditions, implying cultural relationships that likely included the exchange of goods (Drucker 1955). Kwakwaka'wakw elites imported coppers from North Coast groups, which were essential as status markers, and often displayed and even destroyed them during potlatches (Boas 1897; Codere 1990). Kwakwaka'wakw groups produced eulachon oil that was exchanged with Nuu-chah-nulth groups to the south. Other Kwakwaka'wakw exchange products included dried halibut and herring eggs (Codere 1990).

Nuu-chah-nulth wealth goods included abalone and dentalium shell ornaments, large canoes, sea otter pelts, and goat wool blankets. These items were traded, along with slaves, to groups on their northern and eastern peripheries (Arima and Dewhirst 1990; Drucker 1951). A wide variety of other food and nonfood goods including whale products (especially oil), shellfish, dried fish, herring and salmon eggs, and various berries were traded between Nuu-chah-nulth communities and sometimes beyond to Coast Salish, Kwakwaka'wakw, and neighboring Makah groups (McMillan 1999). Trading relations were so extensive that a number of trail systems across Vancouver Island remain well known (McMillan 1999).

Coast Salish and Stó:lō groups traded extensively with neighbors on the Plateau to the east as well as with Wakashan-speaking groups to the west and north. Northern Coast Salish groups exchanged smoked salmon, dentalium shell, hides, and fish oil with other Coastal groups and those from the Interior. Lillooet groups exchanged berries, baskets, furs, and snowshoes (Teit 1906: 232). Upriver Stó:lō groups traded extensively with the Nlaka'pamux to their northeast, sending mats, mountain goat wool blankets, dried salmon, and dugout canoes in exchange for berry products and hemp cordage. The upriver Stó:lō also traded dried salmon with downriver groups who provided sealskins, geophytes, fish, and shellfish (Duff 1952: 95). There were close ties by marriages and associated exchange of goods between Central Coast Salish groups (Suttles 1990c).

The Dalles area of the Lower Columbia was a major trade center for Interior and South Coastal groups. Here, Chinookan groups and neighbors aggregated annually to exchange a wide variety of goods as part of gambling, gifting, debt payoffs, and barter (Hajda and Sobel 2013). Food items exchanged by local groups included salmon products, geophytes (especially wapato), occasional whale and other sea mammal products, and occasional products from terrestrial mammals and birds. Nonfood items exchanged included slaves, blankets, canoes, dentalium beads, copper items, axes, and cooking gear (Hajda and Sobel 2013). External goods exchanged for local Chinookan products could include blankets, hides, weapons, slaves, and, during Colonial times, horses, wire, and beads (Hajda and Sobel 2013). Sobel (2006) documents significant movement of obsidian from multiple regional sources into the Chinookan villages.

Hayden and Schulting (1997) propose an exchange network for the Plateau, with northern and southern trade centers existing in the Mid-Fraser and Lower Columbia areas, respectively, and an eastern boundary along the Upper Columbia valley in southeastern British Columbia. While Hayden and Schulting (1997) argue that exchange was structured around elite socio-political decision-making, Rousseau (2004) argues that there was an economic incentive for common people to maintain access to diverse food sources and nonlocal goods, including toolstone. Given the extensive nature of Plateau exchange relationships, it is possible that both arguments may have some validity.

Upper Lillooet (St'át'imc) groups controlled the fishing sites and trade center at *Setl*, the Six Mile Rapids of the Mid-Fraser (Teit 1906; Walsh 2017). The St'át'imc produced salmon products (dried meat and oil), bark cordage, dried deer meat and hides, furs, copper products, mountain goat wool blankets, and dogs (Teit 1900). Archaeological research confirms that they also produced nephrite jade tools (especially adzes) and steatite items (e.g. pipes, bowls, and ornaments) (Morin 2012; Prentiss et al. 2017). Lower Lillooet (Lil'wat) groups produced products more typical of Coast Salish groups, including various wood products, goat wool blankets, and fish oil (Teit 1900). There were also inter-village exchanges within the Lillooet area, as indicated by movement of lithic toolstone that included Arrowstone Hills dacite, various cherts, and Bridge River nephrite and steatite (Prentiss et al. 2017). In return, Lillooet groups received from the Secwepemc hides (deer, elk, and caribou), bark products, bone beads, and berries. Nlaka'pamux groups also produced and exchanged nephrite adzes and anthropomorphic sculptures, many of which were traded to Coastal groups (Hayden and Schulting 1997; Morin 2012, 2015).

Kettle Falls in northeast Washington State was another significant trading site. Similar to the Six Mile Rapids in the Mid-Fraser, Kettle Falls attracted large groups taking advantage of concentrated salmon populations (Ray 1933). Groups aggregating for fishing and trade included the Sanpoil, Nespelem, Kalispel, Coeur d'Alene, Okanagan, Sinixt, Chelan, and Spokane (Ray 1933; Teit 1930). Major goods exchanged included bison hide products from the Spokane and Coeur d'Alene, shell items from western Plateau groups (e.g. Chelan), and geophytes and deer hides from the Sanpoil (Ray 1933). The Coeur d'Alene traded with both Plateau and Rocky Mountains and Northern Great Plains groups. They obtained hazelnuts, soapberries, bitterroot, and salmon from the Spokane. After the introduction of horses, they collected Catlinite pipes, buffalo robes, and feather bonnets from Plains groups (Teit 1930).

As noted, The Dalles area of the Lower Columbia also served as a major Plateau trade center and, like the others, was also a significant fishing locality. Hayden and Schulting (1997) document the presence of Mid-Fraser nephrite and copper items as well as tubular stone pipes in archaeological contexts in The Dalles locality. Hayden and Schulting (1997) also note that The Dalles trade center was of such significance that a trade language derived from Wishram Chinookan was relied upon by those trading in this locality, much like the St'át'imc dominated the Mid-Fraser, and Okanagan (probably also Sinixt) the Upper Columbia exchanges.

5.2 Potlatches and Feasts

Ritualized generosity in the form of feasting, gifting, and its more formalized variant, potlatching, was central to societies of the Pacific Northwest (Figure 19). Feasting and simple gifting were practiced by all groups in the region, while the highly ritualized potlatching events were associated with more select groups primarily from the Central and North Coasts. The potlatch is described by Drucker and Heizer (1967) as a festival put on by a host group for one or more invited guest groups. During the ceremonies associated with the

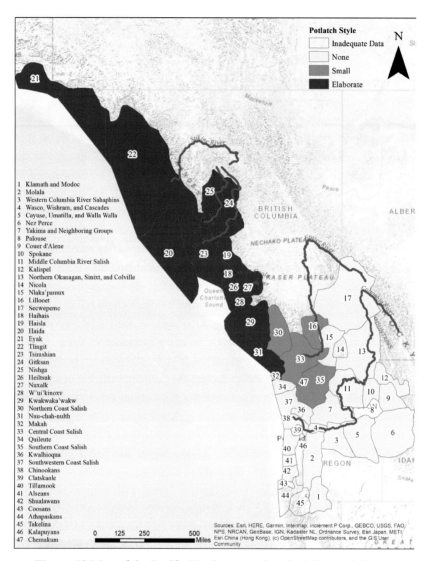

Figure 19 Map of the Pacific Northwest region depicting variation in Indigenous potlatching ceremonies. "Elaborate" means multiple days, extensive gifts, and large-scale feasting (e.g. Hayden 2014).

event, which could last several days and nights, the host group would display their hereditary possessions, which included various items of material culture (e.g. carvings and clothing), songs, and dances. They might also recite stories of their origins and recently transmitted rights. During that process, they could bestow names and associated privileges on select members and then follow with gifts to the invited guests. As noted by Drucker and Heizer (1967), the guests were thus witnesses to claims made regarding individual standing in society and associated privileges. Thus, the potlatch played an essential role in the functioning of society; it could also take on other meanings and provide context for other agendas as associated with the establishment and payment of debt relationships (Hayden 1995). Not surprisingly, it has been of great interest to economic anthropologists.

Codere (1950) provides an explanation for the intensification of production and exchange associated with potlatching amongst the Kwakwaka'wakw that combines historical (Boasian) and functionalist elements. She suggests that, in an environment of extreme abundance, competitive potlatching functioned in place of actual warfare during the Colonial period, in which disease had led to massive population reduction and European trade goods were highly abundant. Suttles (1960) proposed that the potlatch was not a replacement for warfare but rather a functional system by which status was maintained. He recognizes that status brought more productive trade connections and better marriages involving increasingly distant villages. Thus, it was worthwhile to engage in intensive production activities leading to surpluses, which in turn could be given away. Those receiving the presents would then be able to accumulate goods and potlatch back, thus continuing the cycle in every community. Vayda (1961) and Piddocke (1965) argue that it was not the drive for status and its benefits that drove the potlatching cycle but rather the need to even out variation in access to food resources. In their system, environmental fluctuations are the independent variable such that when one social group (e.g. Kwakwaka'wakw numayms) is short on food they sell blankets to the other. The other in turn then accumulates a surplus and puts on more potlatches, giving bigger and better gifts to the former. The former accumulates gifts and can either potlatch back or purchase food at the risk of losing status. But if the latter group falls on hard times, the cycle begins again with reversed roles. Weinberg (1965) builds on Vayda (1961) in asking whether the achievement of plenty in each group might reduce the need to redistribute goods. To answer that question, she proposes that since redistribution in good times is not required, chiefly status would need to be maintained via the sharing of chiefly surplus, made possible by the production by lower-status persons in service of a hereditary chief. This in turn would stimulate specialist crafting, leading to reduced fluctuations in the access to cultural goods. Hayden (1995, 2014) looks to the actions of self-interested elites using feasts and potlatching for purposes of debt manipulation and status aggrandizement. Boone (1998) sees feasting and gifting as signals to attract new membership for house groups fearing demographic loss and associated economic crises. Boone is in line with other scholarship suggesting that long-lived Houses needed to be concerned with demography across cycles spanning centuries (Ames 2006).

Groups located on the North and Outer Central Coasts had elaborate feasting and gifting events (potlatching) that typically incorporated the accumulation and exchange of significant quantities of goods. The Kwakwaka'wakw ritual economy has been most widely discussed by anthropologists (e.g. Boas 1897, 1920, 1966; Codere 1950, 1956, 1957, 1990; Drucker 1941, 1950; Drucker and Heizer 1967). Potlatches and feasts on many scales were designed to legitimize major and minor life events. The potlatch also represented the focus of an investment system whereby loans were taken and repaid. Potlatches and associated feasts were given for naming, taking an important name or position, erasing shame, erecting crest poles, and marriages.

The Tlingit potlatch could be held for many reasons, including memorials, house building, or life event for a young person. However, as noted by Oberg (1973), a potlatch could be offered if a house, clan, or individual felt wealthy enough to hold one. Tlingit potlatches could pay off debt, validate new status, and derive fame. They could also be competitive in the sense that rival clans could compete within a potlatch hosted by a third party. Gift-giving was not competitive, though the gifting system was underlain by a system of loans and repayment (de Laguna 1972, 1990). Tsimshian feasts and potlatches were designed to ritually reinforce social relationships. As noted by Garfield (1939), the potlatch was central to all aspects of an individual's social life whether in terms of validating social standing or affecting economic wherewithal. Tsimshian potlatches could be facilitated by family and lineage group cooperation in the form of donated goods and food. Food provided to feasts associated with potlatches could come in enough quantity to be saved for other uses later (consumption or redistribution) (Halpin and Seguin 1990). The Haida held two kinds of potlatches, a great potlatch for a house-raising and various social changes and achievements and a lesser potlatch associated with raising a mortuary pole (Swanton 1905). Haida potlatches thus validated status and were underlain by complex debt systems, as generally with other North Coast groups. West Coast groups (Nuu-chah-nulth and Makah) produced a similar range of goods for trade and gifting but could also include whale products. Most Nuu-chah-nulth potlatches and feasts were designed to legitimize claims of status, forestall hostilities, create alliances, and hold a following. Unlike some North Coast groups, they were generally noncompetitive unless to compete with an ancestor or, in the case of the *nūcmīs* potlatch, to compete with chiefs of other "tribes" (Drucker 1951: 382).

Groups with smaller communities and few craft specialists generally did not hold large-scale potlatch events. The Coeur d'Alene held a potlatch-like event in which a person, family, and a group of families would identify another individual or group and host them at a three-to-four-day event that included feasting and gifts of hides and horses. The invited person or group would invite the original group for a complementary event (Teit 1930). The Okanagan and related groups (e.g. Sinixt) appear to have held similar small-scale events where families feasted one another with presents (Teit 1930), though the archaeological record suggests that larger-scale events may have occurred in pre-Colonial times (Goodale et al. 2022). Teit (1909) notes that potlatches were unknown amongst the Secwepemc prior to the mid-nineteenth century, when this practice spread into the Fraser River and Lakes Bands.

The Lillooet, Stó:lō, Cowichan, and Wishram had greater investment in feasting and potlatching. Lillooet groups produced a variety of food and goods for exchange and as gifts. Lillooet potlatches were noncompetitive in terms of gift-giving and were undertaken to validate names for children, honor ancestors, and develop fame and status for the host (Kennedy and Bouchard 1978; Teit 1906). As elsewhere in the region, feasts often accompanied potlatches. However, the Lillooet engaged in a unique tradition identified as a "scramble," in which a horse or perhaps one or more deer might be dropped into a house through its rooftop entrance to a waiting crowd, which would enthusiastically dismember the animal(s). Kennedy and Bouchard (1978) note that amongst the Lower Lillooet (Lil'wat) the introduction of money changed the scramble such that long sticks with embedded money might be dropped into the crowd instead of animals. Stó:lō potlatched under similar pretexts as with the Lillooet: establishing a new house, naming, and honoring the dead. However, the ultimate reason appears to have been to pay off debts and to establish and maintain social standing. Duff (1952: 88) states that while Stó:lō potlatches were generally noncompetitive, competitive potlatches were not unknown. Cowichan and Klallam potlatches were generally similar to those of Stó:lō groups, given the common membership in the Central Coast Salish cultural grouping (Barnett 1955; Suttles 1990c). Debt repayment and establishing and maintaining social standing were important (Barnett 1955). Barnett (1955) also describes scrambles somewhat similar to those of the Lillooet groups, though the actual item thrown to the crowd might be symbolic of a greater prize such as a horse or boat. Farther south, the Wishram were Chinookan people with similar subsistence economies to the Chinook. They exchanged shell goods, salmon, slaves, and, during Colonial times, horses (French and French 1998). Wishram groups engaged in ritual generosity to validate new names, changes in social status, and weddings as well as to thank guests for attending the associated ceremonies (French and French 1998).

A final set of groups had generally smaller villages yet still maintained higher numbers of specialists, who were engaged in the crafting of items for gifting and exchange, and conducted feasts of various kinds. However, not all of them held potlatches. While Chinookan groups held a variety of ritual events within which gifting was common, they did not hold actual potlatches (Boyd 2013).

The Squamish and Lummi (and other Central Coast Salish groups) operated political economies similar in many ways to the Cowichan and Stó:lō groups and as such included similar crafting traditions, feasting, and potlatching, though they apparently did not engage in scrambles (Barnett 1955; Duff 1952). The Quinault held what are described as both great and small potlatches to mark major stages of a child's life, honor a deceased relative, and obey the command of a wealth guardian spirit. Ultimately, however, the potlatch brought honor to the giver (generally chiefs) and associated family (Olson 1936). While the Quinault potlatches were four-day affairs with extensive feasting and dancing followed by generous gifting, they are not described as competitive in the way some North Coast potlatch systems operated (Olson 1936). The Quileute held potlatches for validating changes in status and initiations into secret societies. A smaller-scale feast described by Powell (1990) as potlatch-like could be held for weddings, births, naming, coming of age, memorials to the dead, and making a claim to property rights. As with the Quinault, the potlatch served to achieve and reinforce status by providing the feast, gifts, and recitation of heritage (Powell and Jensen 1976). Despite holding a variety of dances (including winter ceremonials typical of most Northwest Coast groups) and other ritual events, potlatching does not appear to have been an important tradition to Tillamook groups (Seaburg and Miller 1990). Coosan groups had similar production and consumption economies to their neighbors, the Tillamook. Like those groups, they also engaged in large-scale ceremonies involving feasting but without potlatching (Jacobs 1939; Zenk 1990).

6 Economic Development

Archaeologists have defined a dramatic long-term history of socio-economic change in the Pacific Northwest region. Here, I provide a short review of major Holocene cultural developments across the region, with particular emphasis on shifts in economic organization. I draw frames of reference from the ethnographic record and from wider thinking about village-scale food-producing societies (Moss 2011). I then follow with thoughts on processes of change as reconstructed on two scales: houses/villages and regional transformations. For the former, I argue that multiple model scenarios drawn from evolutionary ecology and cultural transmission theory are particularly useful. For the latter, I suggest that cultural macroevolutionary theory is of greater appropriateness and consequence.

6.1 Socio-economic Change across the Holocene in the Pacific Northwest

There is clearly considerable variation in economic traditions within the ethnographic Pacific Northwest region. That diversity becomes even greater when we consider the archaeological record. I describe the ancient socio-economic history of the Pacific Northwest in three broad periods that I term simply "Early," "Middle," and "Late" (Figure 20). The Early Period spans the earliest occupations during the terminal Pleistocene to ca. 6000 cal. BP. This was a time of generally low population densities, high rates of residential mobility, and major population movements (Chatters et al. 2012). While probably all groups moved their residential camps on a regular basis, there is evidence that many groups began to establish annual ranges with repeat occupation of key places

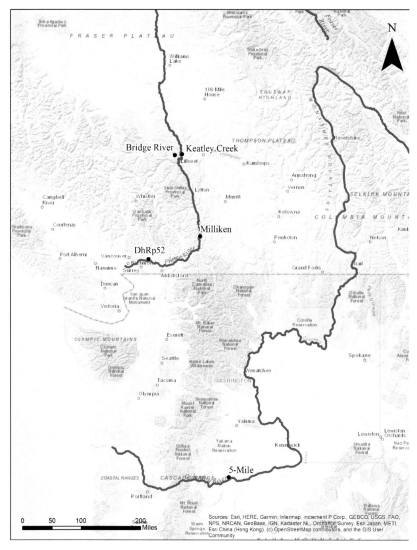

Figure 20 Several major archaeological sites discussed in the text.

(e.g. Chatters et al. 2020). Thus, with the establishment of stable cultural landscapes, we also begin to recognize the intensive use of particular places with predictable high-density food resource. The best examples include the fishing sites at the Five Mile Rapids near The Dalles, Oregon (Cressman 1960), and the Milliken site in southern British Columbia (Mitchell and Pokotylo 1996). On the North Coast, there is also evidence that middens began to accumulate in the Dundas Islands and Prince Rupert Harbour at similarly early dates (Letham et al. 2019; McLaren et al. 2011). The presence of intensively reoccupied fishing sites implies the technological capacity to harvest (with nets) and process fish for immediate and possibly delayed consumption. The degree to which delayed consumption was practiced at these dates remains unclear. Oven technology appears by ca. 7000–9000 cal. BP at the Granite Falls sites near Seattle, WA (Chatters et al. 2020), suggesting that groups may have developed the capacity to mass-process geophytes at early dates. Groundstone tools are generally considered a development that occurred after ca. 5,000 years ago (Ames et al. 2010). However, groundstone items were recovered at Milliken in its early period (ca. 9000–11,000 cal. BP) (Borden 1975), suggesting that the knowledge for making groundstone tools was present long before the practice became common. Finally, small pithouse structures have been dated potentially as early as ca. 6500 cal. BP in the Fraser Valley (Lepofsky and Lenert 2005), also implying that the ability to establish long-term houses was known before the practice was regularly in use.

The Middle Period of ca. 3000–6000 cal. BP was a time of regional diversification in socio-economic developments (Prentiss and Walsh 2016). Small villages with middens and/or house structures appear widely throughout the region, including Haida Gwaii (Mackie and Acheson 2005), the Salish Sea and Fraser Valley (Lepofsky et al. 2009), and the Plateau (Chatters 1995; Rousseau 2004). Beneath the commonality of semisedentary communities was considerable socio-economic variability. Columbia Plateau pithouse hamlets were inhabited by groups employing semisedentism without significant investment in food storage, made possible by the extensive seasonal use of multiple ecosystems (Chatters 1995). Other northern Plateau groups retained a strategy of high residential mobility without investment in food storage either (Prentiss and Kuijt 2004). In contrast, groups on the Coast engaged in diverse resource procurement and processing operations to support growing populations and initial explorations in socio-political complexity. The best-studied example comes from the Lower Fraser Valley and Salish Sea region of the Central Coast. Recent excavations of Charles culture (Matson and Coupland 1995) sites has caused substantial reconsideration of our understanding of socio-economic and political systems. The DhRp52 site in the Katzie area produced what appear to be substantial plank houses and large external ovens dating ca. 4200–5200 cal. BP (Katzie Development Corporation 2014). The house structures and ovens are in line with other Charles sites that have also produced plank houses, ovens, and storage pit features (Ormerod 2002; Schaepe 2003). A large wapato garden was also uncovered at DhRp52 dating to ca. 3800 cal. BP, indicating the intensive production of carbohydrate resources (Hoffmann et al. 2016; Lyons et al. 2021). It is possible that fisheries productivity was increasing at this time, as associated with cooler and wetter conditions of the early Neoglacial period (e.g. Chatters 1995), and thus carbohydrate intensification would have made considerable sense for supporting growing populations (e.g. Tushingham et al. 2021). Intensified food production and investment in housing, large earth ovens, and gardens may also have supported a political economy reflected in outdoor food-related events and the intensive production and exchange of shell and stone beads throughout the local area. Coupland et al. (2016) see the mass-production of beads and the presence of burials with thousands of these items as indicators of emergent material wealth-based inequality. Carlson and Hobler (1993) argue that Coast Salish funerary potlatches may have appeared during this time. Prentiss and Walsh (2016) propose that DhRp52 might have been an administrative center of a polity-like entity minimally on the scale of Nuu-chah-nulth or Kwakwaka'wakw local groups.

The Late Period (ca. 200 to 3000 cal. BP) represents a time when cultural patterns recognized ethnographically became widespread. Large plank house villages emerged in all coastal areas, with particularly well-documented examples in Prince Rupert Harbour (Letham et al. 2019), the Fraser Valley and Salish Sea (Grier 2006; Lepofsky et al. 2009), the west coast of Vancouver Island (McMillan 1999), and the Lower Columbia areas (Boyd 2013). Pithouse villages with storage-based economies emerged on the Plateau slightly before 3000 cal. BP and expended substantially in size after 2000 cal. BP (Prentiss et al. 2005). Most notably, the Mid-Fraser aggregated village phenomenon emerged and expanded after ca. 1800 cal. BP (Prentiss and Kuijt 2012). Populations were supported by intensive production activities facilitated by the extensive management of plants (Turner et al. 2021), shellfish (Lepofsky et al. 2015), and fisheries (Yu 2015). Social inequality as measured on domestic group and House scales appears to have become widespread after ca. 1500 cal. BP (e.g. Ames and Sobel 2013; Prentiss et al. 2007; Prentiss et al. 2012; Ritchie and Lepofsky 2020). Prentiss et al. (in press) argue that clan-based political entities emerged in the Mid-Fraser by ca. 1200–1300 cal. BP. Schaepe (2006) dates rock walls of defensive settlements associated with Upper Stó:lō seasonal polities to within the last 500 years. McMillan and St. Claire (2012) also place the formation of southern Nuu-chah-nulth polities in the last 500 years. Martindale (2003) concludes that while

Tsimshian local groups likely predate European contact, the *Ligeex* paramount chiefdom was a post-contact phenomenon.

6.2 Modeling Economic Change on the Scale of Houses and Villages

Human behavioral ecology, the branch of evolutionary ecology dedicated to the human group, has not been extensively used in the study of economic variation and change within the greater Pacific Northwest, though its influences are growing (e.g. Fitzhugh et al. 2019). Human behavioral ecology offers researchers diverse frameworks for modeling cost-benefit relationships in economic and social strategies (Prentiss 2019). Butler and Campbell (2004), Chatters (1995), Prentiss et al. (2007), and Prentiss et al. ("Malthusian Cycles," 2020) draw on the basic tenets of the diet breadth model to argue that subsistence intensification focused on expanded diet choices is driven by rising search costs for highest-ranked food resources in different contexts of the greater Pacific Northwest. Assuming that anadromous salmon in aggregate represent the top-ranked food item (e.g. Nagaoka 2019), weak salmon runs would lead to foraging decisions favoring wider diet breadth. This could also lead to wider search patterns or extensification across landscapes, as Prentiss et al. (2007) document at the Keatley Creek site in Interior British Columbia.

Access to prey is affected by natural fluctuations in prey populations and prey mobility but also by pressure from human populations (Broughton 1994). Consequently, understanding subsistence decision-making also requires investigation of human population history. Demographic ecology (Puleston and Winterhalder 2019) offers models of demographic change and its impacts on subsistence decisions and human health and mortality. Puleston et al. (2014) provide a model asserting that human communities experience demographic cycles that include growth (copial phase) and rapid transitions to periods of population stasis and reduction termed "Malthusian phases." Among other things, the model predicts that large founding populations, constrained space, and/or low productivity habitat lead to shorter copial phases. In contrast, low founding populations, more extensive habitat, and higher productivity lead to longer copial phases. High rates of mortality (especially the very old and young) and lower birth rates can reduce the length of Malthusian phases. It is also possible that technological innovations might improve subsistence access, thus lengthening copial periods and reducing Malthusian phases (Puleston and Winterhalder 2019). The degree of reliance upon storage can also affect demographic/economic stability in Pacific Northwest villages. Winterhalder et al. (2015) present a model predicting variable storage decisions as mitigation for interannual variation in subsistence returns. In brief, their model suggests that where interannual variation in subsistence yield is low, storage has a very limited effect on human welfare. However, if interannual variation is high, storage can have a major positive impact on welfare. In situations of weak production across multiple years, stores may be exhausted, leading to subsistence crises. However, for some fisher-hunter-gatherer groups, it may be possible to substitute residential mobility and landscape extensification for reliance on storage. Demographic ecological developments also have impacts on human social relations. The demographic ecology models imply that under the sudden onset of Malthusian conditions, human communities could face not just subsistence stress but also emergent competitive conditions within and between their communities. Boone (1992, 1998) argues that under locally variable subsistence conditions it is possible that patron–client relationships could develop as some households come to be reliant upon others, with ensuing loss of status for the former. This could lead select houses to engage in signaling their continued high status via feasting and potlatching with the payoff of attracting vital new members (e.g. Ames 2006) to their houses.

Multi-model scenarios offer an excellent opportunity for addressing complex socio-economic and demographic histories (Prentiss et al., "Malthusian Cycles," 2020). The combined foraging, demographic ecology, and socio-ecological models offer implications for understanding spatiotemporal variation in ancient and pre-modern economies of the greater Pacific Northwest. In theory, we would expect most rapid demographic growth in contexts favoring high-productivity fisheries, for example the cooler and wetter North and Central Coasts (Schalk 1977) and select lower to middle river valleys (e.g. Lower Columbia and Lower and Middle Fraser). High seasonality and interannual variability in many of these contexts would also imply substantial investments in food storage, with implications for subsistence stability and associated demographic trends. Consequently, communities in these highly productive but seasonally and annually variable contexts may have faced potentially significant and recurrent Malthusian demographic phases. In demographically crowded and topographically constrained landscapes, mobility options may have been limited as well. Thus, it would also be likely that social groups (lineages, numayms, and clans, for example) would invest more frequently in competitive (implicit or explicit) strategies (e.g. feasts and potlatches) to attract productive group members while also maintaining and expanding access to local and distant resources (Ames 1995, 2006). This might include intensified subsistence activities and specialist crafting in service of exchange and more frequent ritual events. In contrast, for groups in less productive and less geographically constrained environments (central and eastern Plateau, for example), residential mobility and diversified hunting, fishing, and gathering would replace intensive reliance on the protection of a more constrained resource-procurement landscape. Consequently, there would also be reduced investment in such ritual events as formal feasts and potlatches and less opportunity for craft specialists.

6.2.1 House and Village Change in the Mid-Fraser Canyon 1000–1600 cal. BP

The history of the Bridge River housepit village during the period of ca. 1,000–1,600 years ago provides a good example of these processes in action. The Bridge River site is one of the large Mid-Fraser Canyon villages (Figure 21) that emerged and grew during the centuries shortly after 2000 cal. BP (Prentiss et al. 2008; Prentiss and Kuijt 2012). Given its long history of occupation, it provides a good example of how change occurs as a byproduct of processes acting on House, village, and local group scales.

The Bridge River village (Figure 22) emerged and grew from an initial group of seven pithouses at ca. 1600–1800 cal. BP during the BR1 period to a large village of at least twenty-nine houses during BR3 (ca. 1000–1300 cal. BP). During the BR1 to BR3 periods, the village as a whole persisted through two complete Malthusian demographic cycles. We have identified a slow growth copial period during BR1 and BR2 (1300–1600 cal. BP) peaking in late BR2 with an estimated seventeen co-occupied houses before shifting to a Malthusian phase during which all except three of those houses were abandoned. At approximately 1300 cal. BP, a new rapid growth copial period occurred, leading to the peak occupation, followed in turn by another Malthusian period with a process of steady house abandonment and resulting in nearly complete village abandonment by ca. 1000 cal. BP. Explanation for this demographic history requires insights into regional ecological and cultural trends along with local decision-making. The general trend from small to large village between BR1 and early BR3 parallels regional climate trends that suggest increasingly cool and moist conditions at ca. 1300–1800 cal. BP (Hutchinson and Hall 2019), with marine fisheries' productivity peaking at ca. 1200–1400 cal. BP (e.g. Tunnicliffe et al. 2001). Given that salmon productivity is increased under cooler and wetter conditions (Quinn 2005), we can infer that salmon runs in the Fraser drainage must have been at peak levels during this time. The BR3 demographic decline is also paralleled by indicators of regional climatic warming (Hutchinson and Hall 2019) and a parallel decline in marine fisheries' productivity (e.g. Tunnicliffe et al. 2001). Archaeological data from multiple BR2 and BR3 houses at Bridge River (Prentiss et al. 2014) and nearby Keatley Creek (Prentiss et al. 2007) confirm a general trend from strong to weaker salmon production before and after ca. 1200–1300 cal. BP, development of a wider

Middle Fraser Canyon, British Columbia

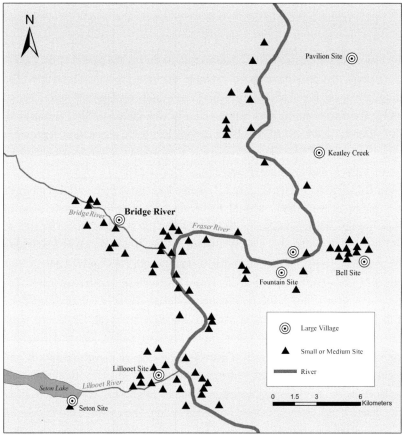

Figure 21 Map of the Mid-Fraser area depicting general locations
of major sites.

diet breadth, and increasingly intensive processing of artiodactyls. Stressful conditions for domestic economies appear to have created the conditions for social
change. Prentiss et al. (2007, 2012, 2014) suggest that Houses with the strongest
economies and most stable populations used feasts and related social events to
attract less well-off persons to join their groups, thus setting the conditions for
emergent inequality as patron–client relationships increased (e.g. Boone 1992,
1998). It is possible that these new ideas regarding approaches to managing
Houses may have been shared around the region after ca. 1500 cal. BP, given that

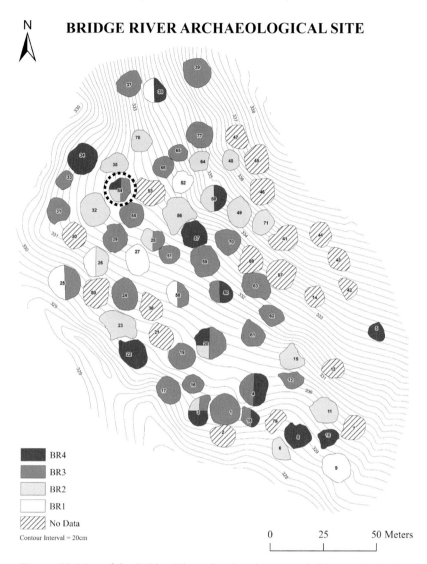

Figure 22 Map of the Bridge River site showing occupied housepits during major occupation periods. Housepit 54 is circled.

similar changes happened in other places at about the same time (Ritchie and Lepofsky 2020). However, village-scale data obscure many critical details of the socio-economic process, including aspects of interfamily negotiations and short-term changes that might only be recognizable with fine-grained intra-house data.

We can gain fine-grained insights into the socio-economic and political processes at Bridge River by considering the record of Housepit 54 (Prentiss 2017; Prentiss et al. 2022). The fifteen-floor sequence (Figures 23–26) spanning the period of ca. 1100–1460 cal. BP at Housepit 54 provides intergenerational

Housepit 54 Stratigraphy

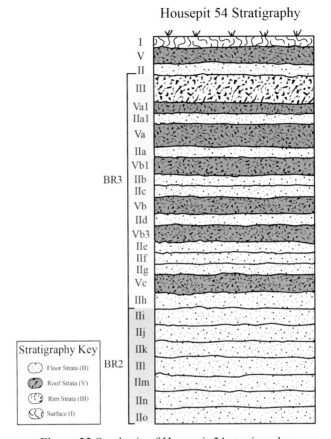

Figure 23 Synthesis of Housepit 54 stratigraphy.

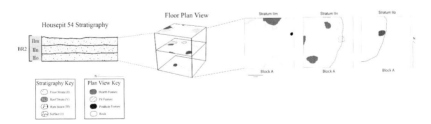

Figure 24 Plan views of floors IIm–o in Housepit 54, Bridge River site.

perspectives on the late BR2 and BR3 periods (Prentiss, Foor et al. 2018). Prentiss et al. ("Evolutionary Household," 2020) argue that the house was occupied by a long-lived House group that transformed its household social relationships during early BR3 times from a communalist to a collectivist strategy. Demographically, the House grew steadily as paralleled by the physical expansion of house size. More specifically, the house doubled in size twice,

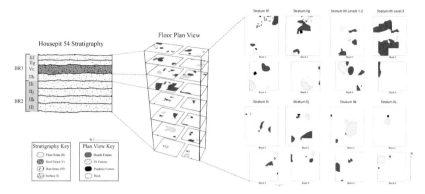

Figure 25 Plan views of floors IIf–l in Housepit 54, Bridge River site.

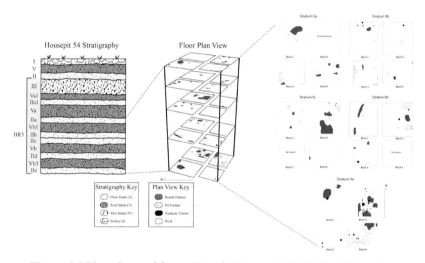

Figure 26 Plan views of floors IIa–e in Housepit 54, Bridge River site.

reaching its maximum extent in early to middle BR3 times (IIe floor). The demographic history is largely paralleled by indicators of overall economic health across the house floors. Relative storage volume peaks on the IIe floor before declining, suggesting that food storage played a major role in supporting household populations through long winters (Prentiss, Foor et al. 2018). Salmon remains are common throughout the stratigraphic sequence but peak on the IIe and IIb floors (middle BR3). Artiodactyl procurement expanded dramatically in early BR3 occupations (peak density on IIf) and persists at generally high levels throughout the other floors, though there is evidence of longer distance transport of elements and more intensive bone grease processing on the late floors (Prentiss et al., "Malthusian Cycles," 2020). There is also evidence that Housepit 54 inhabitants coped with the two Malthusian demographic periods in different ways. The late BR2 population downturn is evident on floors IIi and IIj, where data suggest short winter stays compared to both earlier and later floors. Prentiss et al. ("Malthusian Cycles," 2020) argue that these generations held the house by employing winter residential mobility, one solution for coping with subsistence challenges (Puleston et al. 2014). The mid-to-late BR3 population downturn was managed by developing social alignments that permitted select families to control aspects of food production (possible control of access to best fishing sites and hunting locales) and exchange (as measured by variation in nonlocal and prestigious stone resources). Thus, during mid-BR3 times, Housepit 54 was continuously occupied by multiple families, while only one consistently accumulated large numbers of the latter items and the greatest quantities of artiodactyl remains (Prentiss et al. 2022). Large cooking features and storage pits raise the possibility that these same families periodically held feast-related events.

I suggest therefore that local- and regional-level factors conditioned change in the Mid-Fraser villages. Climate-mediated aspects of subsistence variability cause shifts in fishing, hunting, and gathering strategies. Yet social maneuvering likely also played an important role in determining variation in access to critical resources spanning salmon to deer. Finally, it appears likely that groups employed signaling strategies (spanning display of prestige goods to the use of feasts) to mark status and perhaps attract new membership to the House. Large-scale abandonment of dense aggregate villages may have been a predictable solution to resource imbalances but possibly also a temporary rebuke to conditions of inequality (Prentiss, Foor, and Murphy 2018; Prentiss et al. 2022).

6.3 Long-Term Change in Regional Strategies

Prevailing socio-economies were radically transformed during the period of ca. 3,000–5,000 years ago from small, residentially mobile groups to semisedentary villagers employing intensive food production and storage. Indeed, the Middle Holocene changes in Pacific Northwest socio-economies embody most aspects of what Szathmary and Maynard Smith (1995; see also Szathmary 2015) term "a great transition." Great transitions are in effect transitions in individuality in which parts functioning independently begin to take on new forms of synergy as associated, for example, with the evolution of multicellular life (Szathmary 2015). When change is this dramatic, it is marked by shifts in the locus of replication and selection, increases in task specialization, and transformation in communication systems. From a cultural standpoint, this means that we would expect, first, dramatically new forms of group cooperation

such that group membership becomes crucial for personal economic and reproductive success; second, a diversifying of task specialization such that not
everyone has the same skills yet all benefit from their performance in various
ways; and third, new communication strategies to arise that might include new
symbolic systems to convey the logic of the new order. Such radical transformations are rare in human history but might include such events as the emergence
of agriculture and state-level organizations. The changes that occurred in Pacific
Northwest cultures may offer a similar scale of transformation. If so, it is also
fair to ask how and why this occurred. Laue and Wright (2019) draw on
complex fitness landscape theory to argue that, in small populations under
low selection pressure, innovations of marginal fitness value will often accumulate over long time spans yet make little difference to wider patterns of
cultural evolution. Consequently, these periods of apparent cultural stasis are
actually productive. Under this scenario, conditions are occasionally favorable
for the integration of multiple innovations as might happen under high human
interaction parameters. When that happens it is possible that selection could
reward emergent forms of organization, causing rapid evolution into a very
different new form.

    While space is inadequate here for a full exegesis of cultural macroevolution in
the Pacific Northwest, there are enough indicators to suggest that the great
transition model may have some validity. The emergence of Houses, villages,
and local groups in the Middle Holocene, as represented at DhRp52 and associated sites, could reflect a shift in locus of selection from individuals and families
to more complexly integrated groups. An increase in task specialization is clearly
evident in the dramatic increase in production of specialized groundstone tools,
beads, and harpoons. The rapid spread of plank houses as the standard for
Northwest Coast housing also implies the need for skills that would be recognized
in ethnographic times to be associated with embedded specialists (Ames 1995).
Finally, communication systems may also have been revolutionized with the
appearance and spread of Northwest Coast art motifs as also recognized as first
appearing in Charles culture contexts (Carlson and Hobler 1993). What is a likely
scenario by which this cultural process unfolded? We see accumulated innovations underlying the economic logic of the Charles culture, including intensified
fishing practices at various sites around the region during the Early Holocene,
Early Holocene groundstone at the Milliken site, an Early Holocene roasting oven
at Granite Falls, and Middle Holocene house forms in the Fraser Valley. Benign
late Middle Holocene environmental conditions (Chatters 1998) may have
rewarded larger and longer-lasting annual gatherings in the Fraser Valley and
Salish Sea area, thus triggering the sharing of innovations. If seasonal gatherings
grew around annually high productive locales, we could also expect economic

and reproductive rewards (and, thus, selection) for new social alignments, cooperation networks, and defended territories (e.g. Dyson-Hudson and Smith 1978). New communication systems in this scenario would have been favored to convey these newly emergent social frameworks and associated belief systems. Once present, we can imagine scenarios by which the new socio-economic strategy spread via cultural transmission of its underlying logic and actual movement of human groups (Chatters 1995; Prentiss et al. 2005). Thus, this scenario represents a multi-scalar selection model somewhat similar to that proposed by Spencer and Redmond (2001) for the rise and spread of Monte Alban in Oaxaca, Mexico, at ca. 2,200 years ago.

7 Future Directions

The traditional societies of the greater Pacific Northwest have been described as anomalous among hunter-gatherers, given that they differ from the standard model that includes high rates of residential mobility, egalitarian social relations, aggregation and dispersal cycles, and common property regimes (Lee and Daly 1999). In contrast, Pacific Northwest groups were often sedentary to semisedentary, nonegalitarian, and highly territorial. Arnold et al. (2016) argue that anthropologists and archaeologists have often avoided recognition of such groups, given their divergences from standard expectations of hunter-gatherers. They join others (e.g. Hayden et al. 1985; Prentiss and Kuijt 2004; Sassaman 2004) in recognizing the Pacific Northwest groups as complex hunter-gatherers and thus better aligned with such groups as the Aleut/Unangan, Chumash, and Calusa than the classic mobile hunter-gatherers of the Kalahari, Australian deserts, and American Great Basin. Moss (2011) takes this argument one step further in suggesting that the term "complex hunter-gatherer" should be replaced with "food producer" given the widespread use of intensive food and goods production in Indigenous Pacific Northwest societies that in many ways more greatly resembles that of farming groups than hunter-gatherers. Moss' argument is reinforced by recent evidence that Northwest groups actively managed their ecosystems, encouraging productivity by translocating and managing plants (Turner et al. 2021), creating productive shellfish habitat (Lepofsky et al. 2015), and gardening (Hoffmann et al. 2016). Given the defensible resources, locally dense populations, and the ability to transmit property between generations, it makes sense that high rates of material wealth-based inequality are recognized (Mattison et al. 2016).

It is also no surprise that scholars have promoted a wide range of models seeking to understand the development of Northwest regional cultural traditions. Scholars have long recognized the importance of anadromous salmon as the critical keystone resource underlying dense population and socio-economic and political complexity throughout the region (e.g. Codere 1950; Suttles 1968). Schalk (1977) clarified this position, noting the importance of intensity and predictability in salmon runs as a defining factor associated with the ability of Northwest Coast groups to support dense aggregations with complex economies. Many others have pointed to proximate causes for aggregation, territoriality, and long-distance exchange (e.g. Chatters 2004; Croes and Hackenberger 1988; Matson 1983; Lepofsky et al. 2005). Others have been more interested in prime movers underlying emergent social inequality (Hayden 1994; Johnson 1982). With the exception of Hayden, all recognize the importance of demographic factors in the process of establishing dense aggregate settlements with defended territories, long-distance exchange, and complex ritual economies. The demographic ecology model shows strong potential for insights that do incorporate the range of variation in socio-economic strategies in ecological context. In this framework, we might understand complex social networks and intensified ritual economies in many Coastal and western Plateau groups as evolved strategies for attracting membership in Houses and maintaining long-distance options for access to food and goods during inevitable times of demographic stress where mobility options are largely foreclosed. In contrast, limited investment in specialist production and ritual economy by central and eastern Plateau groups is better understood as a consequence of groups investing in residential mobility and food caching (e.g. Chatters 1995, 2004) across the landscape as a more efficient option to seasonal variation in resources. Thus, it makes economic sense that Haida and Tlingit groups maintained a complex system of clans and moieties while other groups including the Tsimshian, Kwakwaka'wakw, Nuu-chah-nulth, some Coast Salish, and Lillooet groups formed more complex political entities, with others on the Plateau and South Coast avoiding clans and polities altogether. Testing this model will require long-term investment in research into the relationships between regional processes, villages, and household histories (e.g. Prentiss et al. 2014; Prentiss et al., "Malthusian Cycles," 2020).

Multi-model scenarios drawn from evolutionary ecology help us to understand the economic underpinnings of cultural variation in the Pacific Northwest. However, they are not sufficient for fully understanding long-term cultural evolutionary processes as applied to socio-economic strategies. Recent research has substantially altered our understanding of technological and organizational innovations throughout the region. Technological capacity for fisheries and plant intensification appeared in the Early Holocene. Geophyte intensification via intensive crop management emerged in the Middle Holocene (Hoffmann et al. 2016). The latter coincided with the advent of permanent villages with plank houses, food storage, specialist production, and public ritual at least in some areas (Coupland et al. 2016; Lyons et al. 2021). Subsequent changes were structured around innovations made at these early times. This suggests Northwest regional groups were inveterate niche constructors from early dates and, as such, future explanations for long-term socio-economic change will require consideration of concepts of niche construction and ecological inheritance (Zeder 2017). We will benefit from research into the domestication process as associated with dogs (Crockford and Pye 1997; Prentiss et al. 2021) and intensively manipulated plant foods including wapato and camas. Achieving deeper understandings of ancient and pre-modern socio-economic and political variability in the region will also depend on research collaborations between universities, heritage consultants, government archaeologists, and Indigenous groups, as has been demonstrated, for example, by Lepofsky et al. (2009, 2015), Lyons et al. (2021), Prentiss (2017), and Prentiss et al. (2022).

References

Acheson, S., (1991). In the Wake of the Ya'aats'xaatgaay ("Iron People"): A Study of Changing Settlement Strategies among the Kunghit Haida. Ph.D. dissertation, University of Oxford.

Alexander, D., (1992). Prehistoric Land Use in the Mid-Fraser Area Based on Ethnographic Data. In B. Hayden, ed., *A Complex Culture of the British Columbia Plateau*. Vancouver: University of British Columbia Press, pp.99–176.

Alexander, D., (2000). Pithouses on the Interior Plateau of British Columbia: Ethnographic Evidence and Interpretation of the Keatley Creek Site. In B. Hayden, ed., *The Ancient Past of Keatley Creek, Volume 2: Socioeconomy*. Burnaby, BC: SFU Archaeology Press,pp. 29–66.

Ames, C. J. H., Costopoulos, A., and Wren, C. D., (2010). 8,000 Years of Technological Change in the Gulf of Georgia: Is There a Major Transition at 4850 Cal. B.P.? *Canadian Journal of Archaeology* 34, 32–63.

Ames, K. M., (1995). Chiefly Power and Household Production on the Northwest Coast. In T. D. Price and G. M. Feinman, eds., *Foundations of Social Inequality*. New York: Plenum, pp. 155–188.

Ames, K. M., (2002). Going by Boat: The Forager-Collector Continuum at Sea. In J. Habu and B. Fitzhugh, eds., *Beyond Foraging and Collecting: Evolutionary Change in Hunter-Gatherer Settlement Systems*. New York: Kluwer Academic and Plenum, pp. 19–52.

Ames, K. M., (2006). Thinking about Household Archaeology on the Northwest Coast. In E. A. Sobel, D. A. T. Gahr, and K. M. Ames, eds., *Household Archaeology on the Northwest Coast*. Archaeological Series 16. Ann Arbor, MI: International Monographs in Prehistory, pp. 16–36.

Ames, K. M. and Maschner, H. D. G., (1999). *Peoples of the Northwest Coast: Their Archaeology and Prehistory*. London: Thames & Hudson.

Ames, K. M. and Sobel E. A., (2013). Houses and Households. In R. T. Boyd, K. M. Ames, and T. A. Johnson, eds., *Chinookan Peoples of the Lower Columbia*, Seattle: University of Washington Press, pp. 125–145.

Arima, E. and Dewhirst, J., (1990). Nootkans of Vancouver Island. In W. Suttles, ed., *Handbook of North American Indians, Volume 7: Northwest Coast*. Washington, DC: Smithsonian Institution, pp. 391–411.

Arnold, J., (1993). Labor and the Rise of Complex Hunter-Gatherers. *Journal of Anthropological Archaeology* 12, 75–119.

Arnold, J. E., Sunell, S., Nigra et al., (2016). Entrenched Disbelief: Complex Hunter-Gatherers and the Case for Inclusive Cultural Evolutionary Thinking. *Journal of Archaeological Method and Theory* 23, 448–499.

Barnett, H. G., (1955). *The Coast Salish of British Columbia*. University of Oregon Monographs, Studies in Anthropology No. 4. Eugene: University of Oregon.

Barsh, R. L., Jones, J. M., and Suttles, W., (2006). History, Ethnography, and Archaeology of the Coast Salish Wooly-Dog. In L. M. Snyder and E. A. Moore, eds., *Dogs and People in Social, Working, Economic, or Symbolic Interaction*. Oxford: Oxbow Books, pp. 1–11.

Binford, L. R., (1980). Willow Smoke and Dogs' Tails: Hunter-Gatherer Settlement Systems and Archaeological Site Formation. *American Antiquity* 45, 4–20.

Binford, L. R., (2001). Constructing Frames of Reference: An Analytical Method for Archaeological Theory Building Using Ethnographic Data Sets. Berkeley: University of California Press.

Blackman, M. B., (1990). Haida: Traditional Culture. In W. Suttles, ed., *Handbook of North American Indians, Volume 7: Northwest Coast*. Washington, DC: Smithsonian Institution, pp. 240–260.

Boas, F., (1897). *The Social Organization and the Secret Societies of the Kwakiutl Indians*. Washington, DC: Smithsonian Institution.

Boas, F., (1911–1914). *Ethnology of the Kwakiutl, Based on Data Collected by George Hunt: Part I*. Thirty-Fifth Report of the Bureau of American Ethnology, Smithsonian Institution, Washington DC, pp. 43–794.

Boas, F., (1920). The Social Organization of the Kwakiutl. *American Anthropologist* 22, 111–126.

Boas, F., (1966). *Kwakiutl Ethnography*. Chicago, IL: University of Chicago Press.

Boone, J. L., (1992). Competition, Conflict, and the Development of Social Hierarchies. In E. A. Smith and B. Winterhalder, eds., *Evolutionary Ecology and Human Behavior*. New York: Aldine de Gruyter, pp. 301–338.

Boone, J. L., (1998). The Evolution of Magnanimity: When Is It Better to Give Than to Receive? *Human Nature* 9, 1–21.

Borden, C. E., (1975). Origins and Development of Early Northwest Coast Culture to about 3000 B.C. National Museum of Man Mercury Series, Archaeological Survey of Canada Paper No. 45, Ottawa.

Boyd, R. T., (2013). Lower Columbia Chinookan Ceremonialism. In R. T. Boyd, K. M. Ames, and T. A. Johnson, eds., *Chinookan Peoples of the Lower Columbia*. Seattle: University of Washington Press, pp. 181–198.

Broughton, J. M., (1994). Late Holocene Resource Intensification in the Sacramento Valley, California: The Vertebrate Evidence. *Journal of Archaeological Science* 21, 501–514.

Brumfiel, E. M. and Earle, T. K., (1987). Specialization, Exchange, and Complex Societies: An Introduction. In E. M. Brumfiel and T. K. Earle, eds., *Specialization, Exchange, and Complex Societies*. Cambridge: Cambridge University Press, pp. 1–9.

Butler, V. L. and Campbell, S. K., (2004). Resource Intensification and Resource Depression in the Pacific Northwest of North America: A Zooarchaeological Review. *Journal of World Prehistory* 18, 327–405.

Carlson, R. L. and Hobler, P. M., (1993). The Pender Canal Excavations and the Development of Coast Salish Culture. *BC Studies* 99, 25–52.

Chatters, J. C., (1989). The Antiquity of Economic Differentiation within Households in the Puget Sound Region, Northwest Coast. In S. MacEachern, D. Archer, and R. Garvin, eds., *Households and Communities*. Calgary, AB: University of Calgary Archaeological Association, pp. 168–178.

Chatters, J. C., (1995). Population Growth, Climatic Cooling, and the Development of Collector Strategies on the Southern Plateau, Western North America. *Journal of World Prehistory* 9, 341–400.

Chatters, J. C., (1998). Environment. In D. E. Walker Jr., ed., *Handbook of North American Indians, Volume 12: Plateau*. Washington, DC: Smithsonian Institution, pp.29–48.

Chatters, J. C., (2004). Safety in Numbers: Conflict and Village Settlement on the Plateau. In W. C. Prentiss and I. Kuijt, eds., *Complex Hunter-Gatherers: Evolution and Organization of Prehistoric Communities on the Plateau of Northwestern North America*. Salt Lake City: University of Utah Press, pp. 67–83.

Chatters, J. C., Cooper, J. B., and LeTouneau, P. D., (2020). *Hunters of the Mid-Holocene Forest: Old Cordilleran Culture Sites at Granite Falls, Washington*. University of Utah Anthropological Papers No. 134. Salt Lake City: University of Utah Press.

Chatters, J. C., Hackenberger, S., Prentiss, A. M., and Thomas, J.-L., (2012). The Paleoindian to Archaic Transition in the Pacific Northwest. In C. B. Bousman and B. J. Vierra, eds., *From the Pleistocene to the Holocene: Human Organization and Cultural Transformations in Prehistoric North America*. College Station, TX: Texas A&M Press, pp. 37–66.

Clark, T., (2010). Rewriting Marpole: The Path to Cultural Complexity in the Gulf of Georgia. Ph.D. dissertation, University of Toronto.

Codere, H., (1950). *Fighting with Property: A Study of Kwakiutl Potlatching and Warfare 1762–1930*. Monographs of the American Ethnological Society XVIII. New York: J. J. Augustin.

Codere, H., (1956). The Amiable Side of Kwakiutl Life: The Potlatch and the Play Potlatch. *American Anthropologist* 58, 334–351.

Codere, H., (1957). Kwakiutl Society: Rank without Class. *American Anthropologist* 59, 473–486.

Codere, H., (1990). Kwakiutl: Traditional Culture. In W. Suttles, ed., *Handbook of North American Indians, Volume 7: Northwest Coast*. Washington, DC: Smithsonian Institution, pp. 359–377.

Costin, C. L., (1991). Craft Specialization: Issues in Defining, Documenting, and Explaining the Organization of Production. In M. B. Schiffer, ed., *Archaeological Method and Theory*, Tucson: University of Arizona Press, pp. 1–56.

Coupland, G., (1985). Household Variability and Status Differentiation at Kitselas Canyon. *Canadian Journal of Archaeology* 9, 39–56.

Coupland, G., (2006). A Chief's House Speaks: Communicating Power on the Northern Northwest Coast. In E. A. Sobel, D. A. T. Gahr, and K. M. Ames, eds., *Household Archaeology on the Northwest Coast*. Archaeological Series 16. Ann Arbor, MI: International Monographs in Prehistory, pp. 80–96.

Coupland, G., Bilton, D., Clark, T. et al., (2016). A Wealth of Beads: Evidence for Material Wealth-Based Inequality in the Salish Sea Region 4000–3500 CAL B.P. *American Antiquity* 81, 294–315.

Coupland, G., Clark, T., and Palmer, A., (2009). Hierarchy, Communalism, and the Spatial Order of Northwest Coast Plank Houses: A Comparative Study. *American Antiquity* 74, 77–106.

Coupland, G., Steward, K., and Patton, K., (2010). Do You Never Get Tired of Salmon? Evidence for Extreme Salmon Specialization at Prince Rupert Harbour, British Columbia. *Journal of Anthropological Archaeology* 29, 189–207.

Cowan, I. M. and Guiguet, C. J., (1973). *The Mammals of British Columbia*. British Columbia Provincial Museum Handbook 11, Victoria.

Cressman, L. S., (1960). Cultural Sequences at The Dalles, Oregon: A Contribution to Pacific Northwest Prehistory. *Transactions of the American Philosophical Society* 50(10).

Crockford, S. J. and Pye, C. J., (1997). Forensic Reconstruction of Prehistoric Dogs from the Northwest Coast. *Canadian Journal of Archaeology* 21, 149–153.

Croes, D. R. and Hackenberger, S., (1988). Hoko River Archaeological Complex: Modeling Prehistoric Northwest Coast Economic Evolution. In B. L. Isaac, ed., *Prehistoric Economies of the Pacific Northwest Coast*. Research in Economic Anthropology Supplement 3. Greenwich, CT: JAI Press, pp. 19–86.

Darwent, J., (1998). *The Prehistoric Use of Nephrite on the British Columbia Plateau*. Burnaby, BC: SFU Archaeology Press.

De Laguna, F., (1972). *Under Mount Saint Elias: The History and Culture of the Yakutat Tlingit*. 3 parts. Smithsonian Contributions to Anthropology No. 7. Washington, DC: Smithsonian Institution.

De Laguna, F., (1990). Tlingit. In W. Suttles, ed., *Handbook of North American Indians, Volume 7: Northwest Coast*. Washington, DC: Smithsonian Institution, pp. 203–228.

De Laguna, F., Ridell, F. A., McGeein, D. F. et al., (1964). *Archeology of the Yakutat Bay Area, Alaska*. Bureau of American Ethnology Bulletin No. 192. Washington, DC: Smithsonian Institution.

Donald, L., (1997). *Aboriginal Slavery on the Northwest Coast of North America*. Berkeley: University of California Press.

Drucker, P., (1941). *Kwakiutl Dancing Societies*. Anthropological Records 2. Berkley: University of California Publications, pp. 201–230.

Drucker, P., (1950). *Culture Element Distributions, Volume 26: Northwest Coast*. Anthropological Records 9. Berkley: University of California Publications, pp. 157–294.

Drucker, P., (1951). *The Northern and Central Nootkan Tribes*. Bureau of American Ethnology Bulletin No. 144. Washington, DC: Smithsonian Institution.

Drucker, P., (1955). *Indians of the Northwest Coast*. American Museum of Natural History Anthropological Handbook No. 10. New York: McGraw-Hill.

Drucker, P., (1965). *Cultures of the North Pacific Coast*. San Francisco, CA: Chandler Publishing.

Drucker, P. and Heizer, R. F., (1967). *To Make My Name Good: A Reexamination of the Southern Kwakiutl Potlatch*. Berkeley: University of California Press.

Duff, W., (1952). *The Upper Stalo Indians of the Fraser River of B.C.* Anthropology in British Columbia Memoir No. 1. Victoria: British Columbia Provincial Museum.

Dyson-Hudson, R. and Smith, E. A., (1978). Human Territoriality: An Ecological Reassessment. *American Anthropologist* 80, 21–41.

Ellen, R., (1982). *Environment, Subsistence and System: The Ecology of Small-Scale Social Formations*. Cambridge: Cambridge University Press.

Ellis, D. V., (2013). Cultural Geography of the Lower Columbia. In R. T. Boyd, K. M. Ames, and T. A. Johnson, eds., *Chinookan Peoples of the Lower Columbia*. Seattle: University of Washington Press, pp. 42–62.

Fitzhugh, B., Butler, V. L., Bovy, K. M., and Etnier, M. A., (2019). Human Ecodynamics: A Perspective for the Study of Long-Term Change in Socioecological Systems. *Journal of Archaeological Science: Reports* 23, 1077–1094.

Fladmark, K. R., (1973). The Richardson Ranch Site: A 19th Century Haida House. In R. Getty and K. Fladmark, eds., *Historical Archaeology in Northwestern North America*. Calgary: University of Calgary Archaeological Association, pp. 53–95.

Forde, C. D., (1963). *Habitat, Economy, and Society.* New York: E. P. Dutton & Co.

French, D. H. and French, K. S., (1998). Wasco, Wishram, and Cascades. In D. E. Walker Jr., ed., *Handbook of North American Indians, Volume 12: Plateau.* Washington, DC: Smithsonian Institution, pp. 360–377.

Garfield, V. E., (1939). *Tsimshian Clan and Society.* University of Washington Publications in Anthropology No. 7, 167–336.

Gillespie, S. D., (2000a). Beyond Kinship: An Introduction. In R. D. Joyce and S. D. Gillespie, eds., *Beyond Kinship: Social and Material Reproduction in House Societies.* Philadelphia: University of Pennsylvania Press, pp. 1–21.

Gillespie, S. D., (2000b). Lévi-Strauss: *Maison and Societé á Maisons.* In R. D. Joyce and S. D. Gillespie, eds., *Beyond Kinship: Social and Material Reproduction in House Societies.* Philadelphia: University of Pennsylvania Press, pp. 22–52.

Goodale, N., Quinn, C. P., and Nauman, A., (2022). Monumentality in Houses: Collective Action, Inequality, and Kinship in House Construction. In L. Carpenter and A. M. Prentiss, eds., *Archaeology of Households, Kinship, and Social Change.* London: Routledge, pp. 177–203.

Grier, C., (2006). Temporality in Northwest Coast Households. In E. A. Sobel, D. A. T. Gahr, and K. M. Ames, eds., *Household Archaeology on the Northwest Coast.* Archaeological Series 16. Ann Arbor, MI: International Monographs in Prehistory, pp. 97–119.

Hajda, Y., (2013). Social and Political Organization. In R. T. Boyd, K. M. Ames, and T. A. Johnson, eds., *Chinookan Peoples of the Lower Columbia.* Seattle: University of Washington Press, pp. 146–162.

Hajda, Y. and Sobel, E. A., (2013). Lower Columbia Trade and Exchange Systems. In R. T. Boyd, K. M. Ames, and T. A. Johnson, eds., *Chinookan Peoples of the Lower Columbia.* Seattle: University of Washington Press, pp. 106–124.

Halpin, M. M. and Seguin, M., (1990). Tsimshian Peoples: Southern Tsimshian, Coast Tsimshian, and Gitksan. In W. Suttles, ed., *Handbook of North American Indians, Volume 7: Northwest Coast.* Washington, DC: Smithsonian Institution, pp. 267–284.

Hamori-Torok, C., (1990). Haisla. In W. Suttles, ed., *Handbook of North American Indians, Volume 7: Northwest Coast.* Washington, DC: Smithsonian Institution, pp. 306–311.

Harris, M., (1968). *The Rise of Anthropological Theory.* New York: Thomas Y. Crowell Co.

Hayden, B., (1994). Competition, Labor, and Complex Hunter-Gatherers. In E. S. Burch and L. L. Ellana, eds., *Key Issues in Hunter Gatherer Research.* Oxford: Berg, pp. 223–239.

Hayden, B., (1995). Pathways to Power: Principles for Creating Socioeconomic Inequalities. In T. D. Price and G. M. Feinman, eds., *Foundations of Social Inequality*. New York: Plenum, pp. 15–86.

Hayden, B., (1997). *The Pithouses of Keatley Creek*. Fort Worth, TX: Harcourt Brace College Publishers.

Hayden, B., (2014). *The Power of Feasts*. Cambridge: Cambridge University Press.

Hayden, B., (2018). *The Power of Ritual in Prehistory: Secret Societies and the Origins of Social Complexity*. Cambridge: Cambridge University Press.

Hayden, B., Eldridge, M., and Eldridge, A., (1985). Complex Hunter-Gatherers of Interior British Columbia. In T. D. Price and J. A. Brown, eds., *Prehistoric Hunter-Gatherers: The Emergence of Cultural Complexity*. New York: Academic Press, pp. 191–199.

Hayden, B. and Schulting, R., (1997). The Plateau Interaction Sphere and Late Prehistoric Cultural Complexity. *American Antiquity* 62, 51–85.

Herskovits, M. J., (1952). *Economic Anthropology: A Study in Comparative Economics*. New York: Alfred A. Knopf.

Hirth, K., (2020). *The Organization of Ancient Economies: A Global Perspective*. Cambridge: Cambridge University Press.

Hoffmann, T., Lyons, N., Miller, D. et al., (2016). Engineered Feature Used to Enhance Gardening at a 3800-Year-Old Site of the Pacific Northwest Coast. *Science Advances* 2, e1601282.

Hutchinson, I. and Hall, M. E., (2019). Chinook Salmon, Late Holocene Climate Change, and the Occupational History of Kettle Falls, a Columbia River Fishing Station. *Environmental Archaeology*. DOI: 10.1080/14614103.2019 .1648118.

Jacobs, M., (1939). Coos Narrative and Ethnologic Texts. *University of Washington Publications in Anthropology* 8, 127–259.

Johansen, S., (2004). Prehistoric Secret Societies. MA thesis, Simon Fraser University.

Johnson, G. A., (1982). Organizational Structure and Scalar Stress. In C. Renfrew, M. J. Rowlands, and B. A. Segraves, eds., *Theory and Explanation in Archaeology*. New York: Academic Press, pp. 389–421.

Katzie Development Corporation, (2014). *Archaeological Excavations at DhRp52, Final Report, Permit HCA 2007–097*. Report on File, Archaeology Branch, Victoria, BC and Katzie Development Corporation, Pitt Meadows, BC.

Kennedy, D. I. D. and Bouchard, R., (1978). Fraser River Lillooet: An Ethnographic Summary. In A. H. Stryd and S. Lawhead, eds., *Reports of the Lillooet Archaeological Project*. National Museum of Man Mercury Series, Archaeological Survey of Canada Paper No. 73, Ottawa, pp. 22–55.

Kennedy, D. I. D. and Bouchard, R., (1998a). Lillooet. In D. E. Walker Jr., ed., *Handbook of North American Indians, Volume 12: Plateau*. Washington, DC: Smithsonian Institution, pp.174–190.

Kennedy, D. I. D. and Bouchard, R., (1998b). Northern Okanagan, Lakes, and Colville. In D. E. Walker Jr., ed., *Handbook of North American Indians, Volume 12: Plateau*. Washington, DC: Smithsonian Institution, pp. 238–252.

Kenyon, S. M., (1980). *The Kyuquot Way: A Study of a West Coast (Nootkan) Community*. Canadian Ethnology Service, Mercury Series Paper No. 61. Ottawa: National Museums of Canada.

Laue, C. L. and Wright, A. H., (2019). Landscape Revolutions for Cultural Evolution: Integrating Advanced Fitness Landscapes into the Study of Cultural Change. In A. M. Prentiss, ed., *Handbook of Evolutionary Research in Archaeology*. New York: Springer, pp. 127–148.

Lee, R. B. and Daly, R., (1999). Introduction: Foragers and Others. In R. B. Lee and R. Daly, eds., *The Cambridge Encyclopedia of Hunters and Gatherers*. Cambridge: Cambridge University Press, pp. 1–22.

Lepofsky, D. and Lenert, M., (2005). *Report of the 2004 Excavations of the Maccallum Site, (DhRk2), Aggasiz, B.C.* Report on File, Archaeology Branch, Victoria, BC.

Lepofsky, D., Lertzman, K., Hallett, D., and Mathewes, R., (2005). Climate Change and Culture Change on the Southern Coast of British Columbia 2400–1200 cal. B.P.: An Hypothesis. *American Antiquity* 70: 267–294.

Lepofsky, D., Schaepe, D. M., Graesch, A. P. et al., (2009). Exploring Stó: lō-CoastSalish Interaction and Identity in Ancient Houses and Settlements in the Fraser Valley, British Columbia. *American Antiquity* 74, 595–626.

Lepofsky, D. S., Smith, N. F., Cardinal, N. et al., (2015). Ancient Shellfish Mariculture on the Northwest Coast of North America. *American Antiquity* 80, 236–259.

Letham, B., Martindale, A., Supernant, K. et al., (2019). Assessing the Scale and Pace of Large Shell-Bearing Site Occupation in the Prince Rupert Harbour Area, British Columbia. *The Journal of Island and Coastal Archaeology* 14, 163–197.

Lévi-Strauss, C., (1979). Nobles sauvages. In *Culture, science et développement: Contribution á une histoire de l'homme*. Mélanges en l'honneur de Charles Morazé. Toulouse: Privat, pp. 41–55.

Lévi-Strauss, C., (1982). *The Way of the Masks*. Seattle: University of Washington Press.

Levy, J., (1992). *Orayvi Revisited*. Santa Fe, NM: School of American Research Revisited.

Loeb, E. M., (1929). Tribal Initiations and Secret Societies. *University of California Publications in American Archaeology and Ethnology* 25, 249–288.

Lyons, N., Hoffman, T., Miller, D. et al., (2021). Were the Ancient Coast Salish Farmers? A Story of Origins. *American Antiquity* 86, 504–525.

MacDonald, G. F. and Cybulski, J. S., (2001). Introduction: The Prince Rupert Harbour Project. In J. S. Cybulski, ed., *Perspectives on Northern Northwest Coast Prehistory.* Mercury Series, Archaeological Survey of Canada Paper No. 160, Hull.

Mackie, Q. and Acheson, S., (2005). The Graham Tradition. In D. W. Fedje and R. W. Mathewes, eds., *Haida Gwaii: Human History and Environment from the Time of the Loon to the Time of the Iron People.* Vancouver: University of British Columbia Press, pp. 274–302.

Martindale, A. R. C., (2003). A Hunter-Gatherer Paramount Chiefdom: Tsimshian Developments through the Contact Period. In R. G. Matson, G. Coupland, and Q. Mackie, eds., *Emerging from the Mist: Studies in Northwest Coast Culture History.* Vancouver: University of British Columbia Press, pp. 12–50.

Matson, R. G., (1983). Intensification and the Development of Cultural Complexity: The Northwest versus Northeast Coast. In R. Nash, ed., *The Evolution of Maritime Cultures on the Northeast and Northwest Coats of America.* Department of Archaeology Publication No. 11. Burnaby, BC: SFU Archaeology Press.

Matson, R. G. and Coupland, G., (1995). *The Prehistory of the Northwest Coast.* San Diego, CA: Academic Press.

Mattison, S. M., Smith, E. A., Shenk, M., and Cochrane, E. E., (2016). The Evolution of Inequality. *Evolutionary Anthropology* 25, 184–199.

McIlwraith, T., (1948). *The Bella Coola Indians*, vols 2. Toronto: University of Toronto Press.

McLaren, D., Martindale, A., Fedje, D., and Mackie, Q., (2011). Relict Shorelines and Shell Middens of the Dundas Island Archipelago. *Canadian Journal of Archaeology* 35, 86–116.

McMillan, A. D., (1999). *Since the Time of the Transformers: The Ancient Heritage of the Nuu-chah-nulth, Ditidaht, and Makah.* Vancouver: University of British Columbia Press.

McMillan, A. D. and St. Claire, D. E., (2012). *Huu7ii: Household Archaeology at a Nuu-chah-nulth Village Site in Barkley Sound.* Burnaby, BC: SFU Archaeology Press.

Miller, B., (1998). Centrality and Measures of Regional Structure in Aboriginal Western Washington. *Ethnology* 28, 265–276.

Mitchell, D. H., (1983). Seasonal Settlements, Village Aggregations, and Political Autonomy on the Central Northwest Coast. In E. Tooker, ed.,

The Development of Political Organization in Native North America: Proceedings of the American Ethnological Society. Washington, DC:American Ethnological Society, pp. 97–107.

Mitchell, D. and Donald, L., (1988). Archaeology and the Study of Northwest Coast Economies. In B. L. Isaac, ed., *Prehistoric Economies of the Pacific Northwest Coast.* Research in Economic Anthropology Supplement 3. Greenwich, CT: JAI Press, pp. 293–351.

Mitchell, D. and Pokotylo, D. L., (1996). Early Period Components at the Milliken Site. In R. L. Carlson and L. Dalla Bona, eds., *Early Human Occupation in British Columbia.* Vancouver:University of British Columbia Press, pp. 65–82.

Morin, J., (2012). The Political Economy of Stone Celt Exchange: The Salish Nephrite Jade Industry. Ph.D. dissertation, University of British Columbia.

Morin, J., (2015). Classification and Typologies of Stone Celts in British Columbia. *Canadian Journal of Archaeology* 39, 82–122.

Moss, M. L., (2011). *Northwest Coast: Archaeology As Deep History.* Washington, DC: SAA Press.

Munro, J. A. and Cowan, I. McT., (1947). *A Review of the Bird Fauna of British Columbia.* Special Publication No. 2. Victoria: British Columbia Provincial Museum.

Murdock, G. P., (1934). Kinship and Social Behavior among the Haida. *American Anthropologist* 36, 355–385.

Nagaoka, L., (2019). Human Behavioral Ecology and Zooarchaeology. In A. M. Prentiss, ed., *Handbook of Evolutionary Research in Archaeology.* New York: Springer, pp. 231–254.

Newman, T. M., (1959). Tillamook Prehistory and Its Relation to the Northwest Culture area. Ph.D. dissertation, University of Oregon.

Oberg, K., (1973). *The Social Economy of the Tlingit Indians.* Seattle: University of Washington Press.

Olson, R. L., (1936). *The Quinault Indians.* Seattle: University of Washington Publications in Anthropology 6,1–190.

Olson, R. L., (1940). The Social Organization of the Haisla of British Columbia. *University of California Anthropological Records* 2, 169–200.

Ormerod, P. L., (2002). Reading the Earth: Multivariate Analysis of feature Functions at Xá: tem (The Hatzic Rock Site, DgRn 23), British Columbia. MA thesis, University of British Columbia.

Palmer, G. B., (1998). Coeur d'Alene. In D. E. Walker Jr., ed., *Handbook of North American Indians, Volume 12: Plateau.* Washington, DC: Smithsonian Institution, pp.313–326.

Piddocke, S., (1965). The Potlatch System of the Southern Kwakiutl: A New Perspective. *Southwest Journal of Anthropology* 21, 244–264.

Powell, J., (1990). Quileute. In W. Suttles, ed., *Handbook of North American Indians, Volume 7: Northwest Coast*. Washington, DC: Smithsonian Institution, pp. 431–437.

Powell, J. and Jensen, V., (1976). *Quileute: An Introduction to the Indians of La Push*. Seattle: University of Washington Press.

Prentiss, A. M., ed., (2017). *The Last House at Bridge River: The Archaeology of an Aboriginal Household in British Columbia during the Fur Trade Period*. Salt Lake City: University of Utah Press,.

Prentiss, A. M., (2019). Human Ecology. In A. M. Prentiss, ed., *Handbook of Evolutionary Research in Archaeology*. New York: Springer, pp. 217–231.

Prentiss, A. M., Cail, H. S., and Smith, L. M., (2014). At the Malthusian Ceiling: Subsistence and Inequality at Bridge River, British Columbia. *Journal of Anthropological Archaeology* 33, 34–48.

Prentiss, A. M, Cross, G., Foor, T. A. et al., (2008). Evolution of a Late Prehistoric Winter Village on the Interior Plateau of British Columbia: Geophysical Investigations, Radiocarbon Dating, and Spatial Analysis of the Bridge River Site. *American Antiquity* 73, 59–82.

Prentiss, A. M., Foor, T. A., Cross, G., Harris, L. E., and Wanzenried, M., (2012). The Cultural Evolution of Material Wealth Based Inequality at Bridge River, British Columbia. *American Antiquity* 77, 542–564.

Prentiss, A. M., Foor, T. A., Hampton, A., Ryan, E., and Walsh, M. J., (2018). The Evolution of Material Wealth-Based Inequality: The Evidence from Housepit 54, Bridge River, British Columbia. *American Antiquity* 83, 598–618.

Prentiss, A. M., Foor, T. A., and Murphy, M.-M., (2018). Testing Hypotheses about Emergent Inequality (Using Gini Coefficients) in a Complex Fisher-Forager Society at the Bridge River Site, British Columbia. In T. Kohler and M. E. Smith, eds., *Ten Thousand Years of Inequality: The Archaeology of Wealth Differences*. Tucson: University of Arizona Press, pp. 96–129.

Prentiss, A. M, French, K., Hocking, S. et al., (2017). Lithic Technology during the Fur Trade Occupation at Housepit 54. In A. M. Prentiss, ed., *The Last House at Bridge River: The Archaeology of an Aboriginal Household during the Fur Trade Period*. Salt Lake City: University of Utah Press, pp. 67–89.

Prentiss, A. M. and Kuijt, I., (2012). *People of the Middle Fraser Canyon: An Archaeological History*. Vancouver: University of British Columbia Press.

Prentiss, A. M., Lyons, N., Harris, L. E., Burns, M. R. P., and Godin, T. M., (2007). The Emergence of Status Inequality in Intermediate Scale Societies: A Demographic and Socio-economic History of the Keatley Creek Site, British Columbia. *Journal of Anthropological Archaeology* 26, 299–327.

Prentiss, A. M., Ryan, E., Hampton, A. et al., (2022). *Household Archaeology at the Bridge River Site (EeRl4), British Columbia: Spatial Distributions of Features, Lithic Artifacts, and Faunal Remains on Fifteen Anthropogenic Floors from Housepit 54.* Salt Lake City: University of Utah Press.

Prentiss, A. M. and Walsh, M. J., (2016). Was There a Neolithic "(R)evolution" in North America's Pacific Northwest Region? Exploring Alternative Models of Socio-economic and Political Change. In N. Sans, ed., *The Origins of Food Production.* World Heritage Papers (HEADS 6). Paris: UNESCO, pp. 276–291.

Prentiss, A. M, Walsh, M. J., Foor, T. A. et al., (2020). Malthusian Cycles among Semi-Sedentary Fisher-Hunter-Gatherers: The Socio-economic and Demographic History of Housepit 54, Bridge River Site, British Columbia. *Journal of Anthropological Archaeology* 59, 101181.

Prentiss, A. M., Walsh, M. J., Foor, T. A., Hampton, A., and Ryan, E., (2020). Evolutionary Household Archaeology: Inter-generational Cultural Transmission at Housepit 54, Bridge River site, British Columbia. *Journal of Archaeological Science* 124, 105260.

Prentiss, A. M., Walsh, M. J., Foor, T. A., O'Brien, H., and Cail, H. S., (2021). The Record of Dogs in Traditional Villages of the Mid-Fraser Canyon, British Columbia: Ethnological and Archaeological Evidence. *Human Ecology* 49, 735–753.

Prentiss, A. M., Williams-Larson, A., and Hampton, A., (in press). Ethnography and the Interpretation of Ancient Socio-political Structure in the Middle Fraser Canyon, British Columbia. In C. Sampson, ed., *Complex Hunter-Gatherers.* Gainesville: University Press of Florida, (in press).

Prentiss, W. C., Chatters, J. C., Lenert, M., Clarke, D., and O'Boyle, R. C., (2005). The Archaeology of the Plateau of Northwestern North America during the Late Prehistoric Period (3500–200 B.P.): Evolution of Hunting and Gathering Societies. *Journal of World Prehistory* 19, 47–118.

Prentiss, W. C. and Kuijt, I., eds., (2004). *Complex Hunter-Gatherers: Evolution and Organization of Prehistoric Communities on the Plateau of Northwestern North America.* Salt Lake City: University of Utah Press.

Puleston, C., Tuljapurkar, S., and Winterhalder, B., (2014). The Invisible Cliff: Abrupt Imposition of Malthusian Equilibrium in a Natural-Fertility, Agrarian Society. *PLOS ONE* 9, e87541.

Puleston, C. and Winterhalder, B., (2019). Demography, Environment and Human Behavior. In A. M. Prentiss, ed., *Handbook of Evolutionary Research in Archaeology.* New York: Springer, pp. 311–336.

Quayle, D. B., (1960). *The Intertidal Bivalves of British Columbia.* British Columbia Provincial Museum Handbook No. 17. Victoria: British Columbia Provincial Museum.

Quinn, T. R., (2005). *The Behavior and Ecology of Pacific Salmon and Trout.* Bethesda, MD: American Fisheries Society.

Ray, V., (1933). *The Sanpoil and Nespelem: Salishan Peoples of Northeastern Washington.* University of Washington Publications in Anthropology 5. Seattle: University of Washington Press.

Renker, A. M. and Gunther, E., (1990). Makah. In W. Suttles, ed., *Handbook of North American Indians, Volume 7: Northwest Coast.* Washington, DC: Smithsonian Institution, pp. 422–430.

Ritchie, M. and Lepofsky, D., (2020). From Local to Regional and Back Again: Social Transformation in a Coast Salish Settlement, 1500–1000 BP. *Journal of Anthropological Archaeology* 60, 101210.

Rosman, A. and Rubel, P.G., (1971). *Feasting with Mine Enemy: Rank and Exchange among Northwest Coast Societies.* New York: Columbia University Press.

Rousseau, M. K., (2004). A Culture Historic Synthesis and Changes in Human Mobility, Sedentism, Subsistence, Settlement, and Population on the Canadian Plateau. In W. C. Prentiss and I. Kuijt, eds., *Complex Hunter-Gatherers: Evolution and Organization of Prehistoric Communities on the Plateau of Northwestern North America.* Salt Lake City: University of Utah Press, pp. 3–22.

Samuels, S. S., (2006). Households at Ozette. In E. A. Sobel, D. A. T. Gahr, and K. M. Ames, eds., *Household Archaeology on the Northwest Coast.* Archaeological Series 16. Ann Arbor, MI: International Monographs in Prehistory, pp. 200–232.

Sassaman, K. E., (2004). Complex Hunter-Gatherers in Evolution and History: A North American Perspective. *Journal of Archaeological Research* 12, 227–280.

Schaepe, D. M., (2003). Validating the Maurer House. In R. L. Carlson, ed., *Archaeology of Coastal British Columbia: Essays in Honour of Professor Philip M. Hobler.* Burnaby, BC: SFU Archaeology Press, pp. 113–152.

Schaepe, D. M., (2006). Rock Fortifications: Archaeological Insights into Precontact Warfare and Sociopolitical Organization among the Stó:lō of the Lower Fraser Canyon B.C. *American Antiquity* 71, 671–706.

Schalk, R. F., (1977). The Structure of an Anadromous Fish Resource. In L. R. Binford, ed., *For Theory Building in Archaeology: Essays on Faunal Remains, Aquatic Resources, Spatial Analysis, and Systemic Modeling.* New York: Academic Press, pp. 207–250.

Seaburg, W. R. and Miller, J., (1990). Tillamook. In W. Suttles, ed., *Handbook of North American Indians, Volume 7: Northwest Coast.* Washington, DC: Smithsonian Institution, pp. 560–567.

Silverstein, M., (1990). Chinookans of the Lower Columbia. In W. Suttles, ed., *Handbook of North American Indians, Volume 7: Northwest Coast.* Washington, DC: Smithsonian Institution, pp. 533–546.

Smith, C., (2006). Formation Processes of a Lower Columbia River Plankhouse Site. In E. A. Sobel, D. A. T. Gahr, and K. M. Ames, eds., *Household Archaeology on the Northwest Coast.* Archaeological Series 16. Ann Arbor, MI: International Monographs in Prehistory, pp. 233–269.

Smith, L. M., (2017). Cultural Change and Continuity across the Late Pre-Colonial and Early Colonial Periods in the Bridge River Valley: Archaeology of the S7istken Site. In A. M. Prentiss, ed., *The Last House at Bridge River: The Archaeology of an Aboriginal Household in British Columbia during the Fur Trade Period.* Salt Lake City: University of Utah Press, pp.226–246.

Sobel, E. A., (2006). Household Prestige and Exchange in Northwest Coast Societies: A Case Study from the Lower Columbia Valley. In E. A. Sobel, D. A. T. Gahr, and K. M. Ames, eds., *Household Archaeology on the Northwest Coast.* Archaeological Series 16. Ann Arbor, MI: International Monographs in Prehistory, pp. 159–199.

Spencer, C. S. and Redmond, E. M., (2001). Multilevel Selection and Political Evolution in the Valley of Oaxaca 500–100 B.C. *Journal of Anthropological Archaeology* 20, 195–229.

Spradley, J., (1969). *Guests Never Leave Hungry: The Autobiography of James Sewid, A Kwakiutl Indian.* New Haven, CT: Yale University Press.

Suttles, W., (1960). Affinal Ties, Subsistence, and Prestige among the Coast Salish. *American Anthropologist* 62, 296–305.

Suttles, W., (1968). Coping with Abundance: Subsistence on the Northwest Coast. In R. B. Lee and I. DeVore, eds., *Man the Hunter.* New York: Aldine, pp. 56–68.

Suttles, W., ed., (1990a). *Handbook of North American Indians, Volume 7: Northwest Coast.* Washington, DC: Smithsonian Institution.

Suttles, W., (1990b). Environment. In W. Suttles, ed., *Handbook of North American Indians, Volume 7: Northwest Coast.* Washington, DC: Smithsonian Institution, pp. 16–29.

Suttles, W., (1990c). Introduction. In W. Suttles, ed., *Handbook of North American Indians, Volume 7: Northwest Coast.* Washington, DC: Smithsonian Institution, pp. 1–15.

Suttles, W., (1990d). Central Coast Salish. In W. Suttles, ed., *Handbook of North American Indians, Volume 7: Northwest Coast.* Washington, DC: Smithsonian Institution, pp. 453–475.

Swanton, J. R., (1905). *Contributions to the Ethnology of the Haida.* Memoirs of the American Museum of Natural History 8(1), 1–300.

Szathmary, E., (2015). Toward Major Evolutionary Transitions Theory 2.0. *Proceedings of the National Academy of Sciences of the USA* 112 (33). DOI: 10.1073/pnas.1421398112.

Szathmary, E. and Maynard Smith, J., (1995). The Major Evolutionary Transitions. *Nature* 374, 227–232.

Teit, J., (1900). *The Thompson Indians of British Columbia*. Memoirs of the American Museum of Natural History, Jesup North Pacific Expedition 1, 63–392.

Teit, J., (1906). *The Lillooet Indians*. Memoirs of the American Museum of Natural History, Jesup North Pacific Expedition 2, 193–300.

Teit, J., (1909). *The Shuswap Indians*. Memoirs of the American Museum of Natural History, Jesup North Pacific Expedition 4, 443–758.

Teit, J., (1930). *The Salishan Tribes of the Western Plateau*. 45th Annual Report of the Bureau of American Ethnology for 1927–1928. Washington, DC.

Tollefson, K. D., (1987). The Snoqualmie: A Puget Sound Chiefdom. *Ethnology* 26, 121–136.

Tunnicliffe, V., O'Connell, J. M., and McQuoid, M. R., (2001). A Holocene Record of Marine Fish Remains from the Northeastern Pacific. *Marine Geology* 174, 197–210.

Turner, N. J., (1998). *Plant Technology of First Peoples in British Columbia*. Vancouver: University of British Columbia Press.

Turner, N. J., (2014). *Ancient Pathways, Ancestral Knowledge: Ethnobotany and Ecological Wisdom of Indigenous Peoples of Northwestern North America, Volume 1: History and Practice of Indigenous Plant Knowledge*. Montreal: McGill-Queen's University Press.

Turner, N. J., Armstrong, C. G., and Lepofsky, D., (2021). Adopting a Root: Documenting Ecological and Cultural Signatures of Plant Translocations in Northwestern North America. *American Anthropologist* 123, 879–897.

Tushingham, S., Barton, L., and Bettinger, R. L., (2021). How Ancestral Subsistence Strategies Solve Salmon Starvation and the "Protein Problem" of Pacific Rim Resources. *American Journal of Physical Anthropology* 175, 741–761.

Vayda, A., (1961). A Re-examination of Northwest Coast Economic Systems. *Transactions of the New York Academy of Sciences, Series 2*, 23, 618–624.

Walker, D. E. Jr., ed., (1998). *Handbook of North American Indians, Volume 12: Plateau*. Washington, DC: Smithsonian Institution.

Walsh, M. J., (2017). Historical Ecology of the Middle Fraser Canyon, British Columbia, during the Nineteenth Century. In A. M. Prentiss, ed., *The Last House at Bridge River: The Archaeology of an Aboriginal Household in British Columbia during the Fur Trade Period*. Salt Lake City: University of Utah Press, pp. 19–41.

Weinberg, D., (1965). Models of Southern Kwakiutl Social Organization: General Systems. *Yearbook of the Society for General Systems Research* 10, 169–181.

Wilk, R. R. and Netting R. M., (1984). Households: Changing Forms and Functions. In R. M. Netting, R. R. Wilk, and E. J. Arnould, eds., *Households: Comparative and Historical Studies of the Domestic Group*. Berkeley: University of California Press, 1–28.

Williams-Larson, A., Barnett, K. D., Yu, P.-L., Schmader, M., and Prentiss, A. M., (2017). Spatial Analysis of the Fur Trade Floor and Roof at Housepit 54. In A. M. Prentiss, ed., *The Last House at Bridge River: The Archaeology of an Aboriginal Household in British Columbia during the Fur Trade Period*. Salt Lake City: University of Utah Press, pp. 182–208.

Wilson, R. L. and Carlson, C., (1980). *The Archaeology of Kamloops*. Department of Archaeology Publication No. 7. Burnaby, BC: SFU Archaeology Press.

Winterhalder, B., Puleston, C., and Ross, C., (2015). Production Risk, Inter-annual Food Storage by Households and Population-Level Consequences in Seasonal Prehistoric Agrarian Societies. *Environmental Archaeology* 20, 337–348.

Yu, P.-L., (2015). *Rivers, Fish, and the People: Tradition, Science, and Historical Ecology of Fisheries in the American West*. Salt Lake City: University of Utah Press.

Zeder, M. A., (2017). Domestication As a Model System for the Extended Evolutionary Synthesis. *Interface Focus* 7, 20160133.

Zenk, H. B., (1990). Siuslawans and Coosans. In W. Suttles, ed., *Handbook of North American Indians, Volume 7: Northwest Coast*. Washington, DC: Smithsonian Institution, pp. 572–579.

Acknowledgments

I thank Tim Earle, Ken Hirth, and Emily Kate for inviting me to write this Element and for their guidance and aid in the writing and publication process. I thank the Native American and First Nations groups of the Pacific Northwest for sharing their important heritage. I especially thank the leadership and members of Xwísten, the Bridge River Indian Band, for their ongoing interest in archaeological research at their ancestral village. I thank Megan Denis, Ashley Hampton, and Ethan Ryan for contributing figures (Figures 1–5, 10–11, 14, 17, 19–20 [Megan Denis], 21–22 [Ethan Ryan], and 23–26 [Ashley Hampton]). I thank Ashley Hampton, Ken Hirth, and three anonymous peer reviewers for their feedback on the manuscript. I thank the National Science Foundation (USA) for supporting research at Bridge River (BCS-0313920, BCS-0713013, BCS-1916701). I thank the National Endowment for the Humanities (USA) for their support of research at Housepit 54, Bridge River site (RZ-51287–11 and RZ-230366–1). Any views, findings, conclusions, or recommendations expressed in this Element do not necessarily represent those of the National Endowment for the Humanities. Finally, I thank the University of Montana for the time and space to work on this project.

Ancient and Pre-modern Economies

Kenneth Hirth

Pennsylvania State University

Ken Hirth's research focuses on the study of comparative ancient economy and the development of ranked and state-level societies in the Americas. He is interested in political economy and how forms of resource control lead to the development of structural inequalities. Topics of special interest include: exchange systems, craft production, settlement patterns, and preindustrial urbanism. Methodological interests include: lithic technology and use-wear, ceramics, and spatial analysis.

Timothy Earle

Northwestern University

Tim Earle is an economic anthropologist specializing in the archaeological studies of social inequality, leadership, and political economy in early chiefdoms and states. He has conducted field projects in Polynesia, Peru, Argentina, Denmark, and Hungary. Having studied the emergence of social complexity in three world regions, his work is comparative, searching for the causes of alternative pathways to centralized power.

Emily J. Kate

University of Vienna

Emily Kate is a bioarchaeologist with training in radiocarbon dating, isotopic studies, human osteology, and paleodemography. Having worked with projects from Latin America and Europe, her interests include the manner in which paleodietary trends can be used to assess shifts in social and political structure, the effect of migration on societies, and the refinement of regional chronologies through radiocarbon programs.

About the Series

Elements in Ancient and Premodern Economies are committed to critical scholarship on the comparative economies of traditional societies. The Elements either focus on case studies of well documented societies, providing information on domestic and institutional economies, or provide comparative analyses of topical issues related to economic function. Each Element adopts an innovative and interdisciplinary view of culture and economy, offering authoritative discussions of how societies survived and thrived throughout human history.

Cambridge Elements ⁼

Ancient and Pre-modern Economies

Printed in the United States
by Baker & Taylor Publisher Services